MW00943331

Beyond All Measure

Wes McMurray

PRESS

Praying that you'll be blessed
by this little book about
our great God.

In Him + For Him,

~~[signature]~~

(Mt. 13:44)

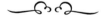

I dedicate this book to my wife, Jennifer.
You radiate the love of Christ.

Acknowledgements

The concept of this book was primarily birthed by my reading through a book called, "All Loves Excelling" by John Bunyan.[1] If you want to read a more thorough book about the same subject, it would be the one to get. While reading through that book, three other significant events happened that helped put this work together.

The first was that Ephesians 3:14-21 became the key passage through which I began to pray over my family. Out of this prayer came a conviction that most of my personal sin is directly related to not comprehending His incredible love for me. In other words, my sins are foundationally being sown in a lack of faith that God's plans for me are what are best for me. When I choose to disobey God, it is a lack of faith that His promises are sufficient and that His plans are good. Thus I choose what I think is best for me. This prayer has helped me grasp the significance of understanding His incomprehensible love for us.

The second event that occurred was that our pastor Eddie Spencer preached a message on this passage. I was struck by the fact that we are called to know something that surpasses knowledge. This doesn't make any sense unless you keep reading into verse 20: "Now to Him who is able to do far more abundantly than all that we ask or think, according to the power at work within us." It is by the power of God that we can pray to know something that surpasses knowledge.

The third event that occurred was that Parkwood Baptist Church asked me to do some interim teaching for the high school students on Wednesday nights. My heart had been so tied to this passage, that I felt God wanted me to share this message with the students at Parkwood. It was from these events that the desire to complete this work was conceived.

Without the help of others, this book would have never been completed. Matthew Little, Kathy Little, David Thurston, Cassie Murray and Ed Martin were extremely helpful and encouraging while I sought to polish my writing. William Haun was responsible for the incredible cover photo and design. My wife has been remarkably supportive and encouraging from the beginning to the end. Thank you! Most importantly, I thank God for loving me in such a way that constantly keeps me amazed.

Contents

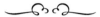

Introduction

"We are never nearer Christ than when we find ourselves lost in a holy amazement at His unspeakable love."[1]
-John Owen

We live in a world that loves to measure things. We measure distance with terms like inches, feet, yards and miles, or by use of the metric system depending on where you live. We use seconds, minutes, hours and days to measure time. Temperature is communicated through Fahrenheit and Celsius to help us know what kind of clothes to wear. Gigabytes and RAM largely determine the worth of a computer. The kitchen is dominated by terms of measurement: teaspoons, tablespoons, cups, fluid ounces, and 'dashes.' It would be difficult to go through a single day without referencing some type of measurement.

I suppose it's no wonder that we carry the notion of measurement over into relationships, even our relationship with God. If settings and circumstances are pleasant and enjoyable, God must love us. However, if things are not going well, we make the false assumption that God does not care for us. We love to measure things, and the love of an unseen God is easily mistaken as paralleled with our surroundings.

Beyond Scales, Scoreboards and Feelings

It is my hope that this book will encourage us to see Christ's love for us in an overwhelmingly immeasurable degree. The scales that measure good versus bad as a barometer for God's love can be stuffed into the garbage. The scoreboards we use to see how others' lives are shaping up compared to ours, as an indication of God's involvement in our lives, can be torn down. The feelings that sometimes are misleading can be encouraged to focus on the joyous truth that God's love is beyond all measure.

The truth is that people want to be loved. They want to know that they are known, cared for, and that someone loves them. The problem with this desire to be loved is that so often our views of love are molded by what we experience in interacting with those around us. Those expressions of love may be accurate, or they may be seriously flawed. There is a love that is pure and undefiled, but it is not found in other people. Ultimately, the love that we long for is found only in God.

This is not a book about how to love one another, although those books are necessary. My mother-in-law has actually written a wonderful book on that subject. She wrote it as the sequel to her critically-acclaimed (by her family) "How to Parent Your Adult Child." Here's how the book reads: "Don't. The End."[2] Her second book was called, "Loving Other People," which reads: "Do it anyway. The End."[3] She's not one to waste words.

The truth is, this is not primarily a practical book, although the foundation for practical living will be presented throughout. This book is about Jesus. This book is about His love (Eph. 3:17-19). It is divided into four parts, corresponding with the breadth, length, depth and height of His love. Under each part, there are two chapters exploring who we are and how Christ relates to us in spite of who we are. The underlying motive of this design is aptly stated by Thomas Watson, "Till sin be bitter, Christ will not be sweet."[4]

My desire is that each of us would expand our view of Christ's love for us. We have but a partial view of His incredible love, and so each of us needs to grow in our knowledge of His love. This will be an eternal endeavor, and so I can think of very little that is more exciting than striving together to grow in the knowledge of the love of Christ.

I'm not the best at trying to illustrate things, and it's a little daunting trying to illustrate something that "surpasses knowledge" (Ephesians 3:19). To put it in the words of John Bunyan, it's like trying to "describe the inexpressible."[5] With that said, I think it's helpful to have some kind of visual to try to understand what I hope to take place within this short work.

In my mind, I picture blowing up a balloon. At some point in blowing up a balloon, there comes a time when you stop for fear that it might explode in your face. I always stopped early because an explosion that close to my face was terrifying to me. I think most of us learn a little of Christ's love, but then stop for fear of what may lie ahead if we learn any more of it. I've been around people enough to know that the "cost" of following Christ is calculated regularly and is often found not worth it.

The balloon in my mind this time has no chance of remaining intact. There is no intention of keeping it intact. I want us to study these Scriptures together with the prayer and purposeful intention of expanding our view of His love to the degree that we don't place any of our previous limitations upon it. We want to bust the seams on our tiny views of His love for us, and I would love for this study to help aid in the process.

The first part of this book will look at the length of God's love for us. It doesn't matter what you've done; His loving arms are long enough to reach you. The second part will look at the breadth of God's love for us. There are no boundaries to His love. This part will address the reality that it doesn't matter who you are or how bad you are; God's love is broad enough to reach you. The third part will explore the depths of His love. No matter how bad things get or how low you feel, the love of Christ reaches to the depths. The last part looks at the height of His love. His love is above all things. He is sovereign in His loving providence of this world. I encourage you to pray through Ephesians 3:14-21 before each chapter:

For this reason I bow my knees before the
Father, from whom every family in heaven
and on earth is named, that according to the
riches of His glory He may grant you to be
strengthened with power through His Spirit
in your inner being, so that Christ may dwell
in your hearts through faith- that you, being
rooted and grounded in love, may have
strength to comprehend with all the saints
what is the breadth and length and height and
depth, and to know the love of Christ that
surpasses knowledge, that you may be filled
with all the fullness of God. Now to Him who
is able to do far more abundantly than all that
we ask or think, according to the power at
work within us, to Him be glory in the church
and in Christ Jesus throughout all generations, forever and ever. Amen.

This is the text that inspired this book. At the
heart of this passage, is a prayer for strength to
comprehend the boundless dimensions of Christ's
love for us. Paul's not suggesting that the Ephesian
people have no understanding of Christ's love, but
he is praying that their understanding would grow in
degree. He describes Christ's love as immeasurable.
There are no pictures that give due justice to His love.
One can't use a concrete measurement to display His
love and then say, "He loves you this much!" All
such descriptions will fall desperately short.
Paul's prayer in Ephesians reveals that one of the
motives for praying to comprehend the love of Christ,

is that we would grow in maturity. This is why he prays, "that you may be filled with all the fullness of God." His love for us produces a response. When one gets a glimpse of Christ's immeasurable love, the response to it is difficult to express. The story is told of R.A. Torrey's experience of praying to see God's face more, until one day while in God's presence, he was so overwhelmed by His love that he began to uncontrollably weep. His weeping continued to the point that he could bear it no longer and he asked God to show him no more.[6] Perhaps, one of the most appropriate and helpful expressions of response is through song. For this reason, I have included the lyrics to a song at the end of each section of the book as a worshipful response.

A couple of years ago, on Valentine's Day, I preached a message about the love of God to students at our church. I used the text 1 John 4:16-17,

> So we have come to know and to believe the love that God has for us. God is love, and whoever abides in love abides in God, and God abides in him. By this is love perfected with us, so that we may have confidence for the day of judgement, because as He is so also are we in this world.

As I prepared that message, I soon began to realize that the word "love" takes on hundreds of different meanings to people. Part of my prayer for that night was that God would help clean our soiled views of love.

When I was young, we used to live in front of a small section of woods. My brothers and I loved to go into the woods with a machete and make trails. My oldest brother, Brian, was the one who usually got to blaze the trail with the machete. It was a lot of work to cut through the undergrowth of trees to make a trail to get to the area where we had found vines on which we could swing. It had been years since I had thought about those days cutting through the forest, but the night that I prepared to speak about God's love on Valentine's Day, those memories flooded my mind. This quickly became my prayer that God would help use the preaching of His Word that night to cut down any mental undergrowth that would prevent us from seeing a clear picture of what it is to be loved by God. Concerning "love," our culture has allowed, embraced, and even cultivated all kinds of "weeds" to grow into what look like deep-rooted trees. The misconceptions of love have taken root in the minds of people, but provide no real root in times of need. So much so, that a proper definition of love is scarcely recognizable.

In the larger context of 1 John 4, the word "love" is mentioned twenty-eight times. But there is a stark contrast to the ideas of love presented by the world and the love "made manifest among us," by Christ (1 John 4:9). Steve Jeffery, Michael Ovey and Andrew Sach have noted this unfortunate mixture of the two completely different views of love:

> Love means very different things to different people, and it can be hard to separate the

biblical wheat from the sentimental chaff. A moment's thought tells us that the half-baked Hollywood caricature needs to be kicked firmly into the long grass...The vague nebulous idea of love so prevalent in our society is very fragile. It serves us well when the sun shines down on us, and life is easy, but it offers no defence against the savage onslaught of personal tragedy...This is a far cry from the strong, powerful love spoken of in Scripture.[7]

I am convinced that when we hear about God's love for us, our minds have a clouded, if not warped view of what that means. Love is often a hollow word used and heard with little thought given to it. In our culture, the idea of "love" is no big deal. D.A. Carson has rightly observed, "Nowadays if you tell people that God loves them, they are unlikely to be surprised."[8] We must not be calloused to this word when considering God's love for us.

Instead of providing a short definition of the word "love," I hope to provide a picture of it through the narratives of Scripture. It is the breadth, length, depth and height of God's love that I hope to explore with this book. If we were to take each of those words and use its opposite, perhaps we could come up with an embarrassing, yet accurate composite of much of the Western Church's idea of God's love: a narrow, brief, shallow and short love. It should come as no surprise when we consider that most of our images of love are characterized by these words.

Our culture's view of love is that in order to be loved you have to be a certain person with a special look. Henri Nouwen writes:

> The world says: Yes, I love you if you are good-looking, intelligent, and wealthy. I love you if you have a good education, a good job, and good connections. I love you if you produce much, sell much, and buy much...The world's love is and always will be conditional.[9]

If the "look" doesn't remain, the usefulness is discarded, and so is the individual. The message is that the worth of a person is seen primarily in their performance rather than the reality that they have been created in the image of God. The display of this love splashes loudly of shallowness.

It's one thing to display that kind of love, but the undercurrent of teaching that this is love magnifies its hideousness all the more. Girls are shown and taught that they will be loved *if* they look a certain way. Guys are taught that love is a feminine attribute, and that real men display manhood by making objects out of women. It is not my goal to write about these issues as much as just provide evidence of the perverted understanding of love in our culture.

How does Christ view our culture in light of this display and inaccurate teaching of love? In Matthew 10, Jesus is going throughout cities and villages, and the Scripture says, "When He saw the crowds, He had compassion for them, because they were harassed and helpless, like sheep without a shepherd" (Matthew 10:36). This is His response to us as well. How does He view a harassed people? He looks upon us with great compassion.

The ultimate purpose behind this writing is that God would be glorified. This is the aim of the prayer in Ephesians 3:20-21: "Now to Him who is able to do far more abundantly than all that we ask or think, according to the power at work within us, to Him be glory in the church and in Christ Jesus throughout all generations, forever and ever. Amen."

Part 1

Think Long[1]

1

How Far Away

"If You, Lord, should mark iniquities, O Lord, who could stand?" –Psalm 130:3

There seems to be an increase in the decrease of thinking. I heard someone point out one time that in the U.S. we are the most entertained people in the history of the world, and simultaneously the most bored. There seems to be an insatiable desire to constantly be amused by movies, ipods, computers, video games, sports, etc... The word "amusement" itself should be an embarrassing word to us since it basically means to "not think." The word "muse" means "to become absorbed in thought."[1] Adding the prefix "a," which is a negative, means to "not become absorbed in thought." In other words, when you go to an amusement park, you're going to a place where you're not going to be required to do much thinking.

Our culture is gorging itself on amusement, and what it has gained is a collective out-loud yawn. We're bored with what we see. The scary part as one author has noted is that "as Christians, our minds are going to waste."[2]

What we find in Scripture is anything but boring! The next two chapters will explore the story of the Prodigal Son from Luke 15. It is one of the most exciting stories you'll ever hear, and it's worth carving out some time to "think long" on the subject of His love.

The purpose of this chapter and the next will be to show that no matter what you've done, you are not beyond the reach of His love. This is the story of amazing grace. Let's pray that we're not unamazed by it.

And He said, "There was a man who had two sons. And the younger of them said to his father, 'Father, give me the share of property that is coming to me.' And he divided his property between them. Not many days later, the younger son gathered all he had and took a journey into a far country, and there he squandered his property in reckless living. And when he had spent everything, a severe famine arose in that country, and he began to be in need. So he went and hired himself out to one of the citizens of that country, who sent him into his fields to feed pigs. And he was longing to be fed with the pods that the pigs ate, and no one gave him anything."

> *"But when he came to himself, he said,*
> *'How many of my father's hired servants*
> *have more than enough bread, but I perish*
> *here with hunger! I will arise and go to my*
> *father, and I will say to him, "Father, I have*
> *sinned against heaven and before you. I am*
> *no longer worthy to be called your son. Treat*
> *me as one of your hired servants."' And he*
> *arose and came to his father. But while he*
> *was still a long way off, his father saw him*
> *and felt compassion, and ran and embraced*
> *him and kissed him. And the son said to him,*
> *'Father, I have sinned against heaven and*
> *before you. I am no longer worthy to be called*
> *your son.' But the father said to his servants,*
> *'Bring quickly the best robe, and put it on*
> *him, and put a ring on his hand, and shoes on*
> *his feet. And bring the fattened calf and kill it,*
> *and let us eat and celebrate. For this my son*
> *was dead, and is alive again; he was lost and*
> *is found.' And they began to celebrate (Luke*
> *15:11-24).*

The story told by Jesus is in response to the Pharisees' reaction to Him "receiving sinners and eating with them" (Luke 15:2). The Pharisees were the separated ones. They didn't associate with the "sinful." The Pharisees treated the sinful as if they had contagious diseases. They focused on the external laws and traditions. The outward appearance was preeminent, and so eating with sinners was viewed as a defilement of the person, as well as giving a stamp of approval to what they were doing.

These people are still easy to find today, focusing on the external commands to the neglect of the heart. The only thing that really matters to these types of people is walking the religious line by strict obedience. God isn't interested in rote obedience. As a matter of fact, God speaks against this type of duty:

> What to me is the multitude of your sacrifices? says the Lord; I have had enough of burnt offerings of rams and the fat of well-fed beasts; I do not delight in the blood of bulls, or of lambs, or of goats…Bring no more vain offerings; incense is an abomination to me. New moon and Sabbath and the calling of convocations- I cannot endure iniquity and solemn assembly. Your new moons and your appointed feasts my soul hates; they have become a burden to me; I am weary of bearing them. When you spread out your hands, I will hide my eyes from you; even though you make many prayers, I will not listen; your hands are full of blood (Isaiah 1:11, 13-15).

Jesus gives the same message to the Pharisees on several occasions:

> Woe to you, scribes and Pharisees, hypocrites! For you clean the outside of the cup and the plate, but inside they are full of greed

and self-indulgence. You blind Pharisee! First clean the inside of the cup and the plate, that the outside also may be clean! (Matthew 23:25-26).

Woe to you, scribes and Pharisees, hypocrites! For you are like whitewashed tombs, which outwardly appear beautiful, but within are full of dead people's bones and all uncleanness. So you also outwardly appear righteous to others, but within you are full of hypocrisy and lawlessness (Matthew 23:27-28).

You hypocrites! Well did Isaiah prophesy of you, when he said: "This people honors me with their lips, but their heart is far from me; in vain do they worship me, teaching as doctrines the commandments of men (Matthew 15:7-9).

It was in this context of this self-righteous attitude that Jesus gives three stories in Luke 15 about how God relates to sinners. The three stories all have several corresponding elements. The first is a story of the lost sheep. The second is the story of the lost coin, and then the last is the story of the lost son. All three stories contain the element of something precious that is lost (15:4, 8, 32), and then the joy that is expressed when that something is found (15:6, 9, 32). We'll now focus out attention on the lost son.

"I Wish You Were Dead"

There are two sons in this story. One is the straight-laced older brother; the other is the rebellious younger brother. In the story, the younger brother comes to the father and asks for his inheritance. In that culture, it would've been the same as saying, "I wish you were dead," or maybe even more accurately, "give me my inheritance now, because I can't wait for you to die." Even in our culture, it would be extremely taboo for one to go to his father and ask for his portion of the inheritance. It's a statement that reveals his interests are in the possessions of the father rather than in the father himself.

We don't know why the son wants to leave, but he does, and he doesn't care how offensive his departure is. He just wants to leave and live his own life away from his father, and not just a little ways off, but to "a far country" (v. 13).

It is the story of my own life. Not that I asked my parents for an early inheritance or for that matter even said hurtful things to them, but in its essence, it is the same. For a long season, I rejected the values and truths that my family had passed down to me and went my own way with what I thought would be best. I'm not too unlike this prodigal son who rejected the goodness of his father to explore things on his own and in his own way. For several years, I tried to ignore the presence of God in my life. It was an effort to at least inwardly go to "a far country" away from His presence.

Looking back on it, I now realize that I was blind to His goodness. When I was younger, I had a relationship with Him. It was in my teenage years that I began to drift away, and the scales over my eyes that hid His love grew thicker. The obvious question now is why would I have run from His tender care?

There's an old movie that I used to watch when I was younger. My father has a thing for the old classic movies, and we owned one called, "Charade." Cary Grant and Audrey Hepburn are the stars of it, and it's a great mystery. The plot is that Audrey Hepburn's husband is killed by someone looking for a treasure that he had. No one knows exactly what the treasure is, but they know that he had it, and that it was worth hundreds of thousands of dollars. Even his wife is clueless as to what the treasure is. As the search progresses throughout the movie, there is one scene in which they pour the deceased husband's bag out onto a bed. Everything he owned was in the bag and in plain sight of the viewing audience. As I watched the film with my father, I said something along the lines of, "Well, it's not in there," to which my father responded with, "You're looking right at it."

"Really?"

"Yep. Something on that bed is worth several hundred thousand dollars and you're looking right at it."

There was nothing on the bed but a few random items, like a key, an envelope, some kind of peppermint powder, and a few other odds and ends. If it was worth that much money, I sure didn't see it. I couldn't figure out what it was, and as I kept watching, I felt as puzzled as those who were searching for it in the movie. About fifteen minutes later, one of the characters is at a carnival and passes by a stamp collector. At that point the light bulb goes off. He realizes that the envelope had stamps on it, and they were rare and probably worth thousands of dollars. Soon, all the characters in the movie realized that this was what they had been looking for, and it was right in front of them the entire time.

I think a lot of people who grow up in Christian homes have a similar experience. The treasure of the glory of Christ is right in front of us, but we miss it. We're blinded to it. Paul writes about this blinding in his second letter to the Corinthians: "The god of this world has blinded the minds of the unbelievers, to keep them from seeing the light of the gospel of the glory of Christ" (2 Corinthians 4:4). It is the intent and purpose of Satan to keep us from seeing the treasure of the glory of Christ. How many have left home to go into a "far country" to seek joy?

The Good Life!

The son takes the inheritance and seeks the "good life," one without restraint or responsibility. The Scripture simply says, "he squandered his property in reckless living" (Luke 15:13). His departure from his father's house was no doubt an exhilarating expression of freedom. He would answer to no one. He would do the things that he had always wanted, but felt harnessed from.

His journey was one of seeking pleasure and satisfaction. Underlying his pursuit was the presupposition that he would be truly happy when he could do whatever he wanted to do. It was the Epicurean philosophy of pursuing what feels good. Epicurus rationally concluded that kissing is more pleasurable than labor, therefore, one should pursue kissing over labor. Those weren't his exact words, but the hedonistic ideas were similar.

The son probably developed a quick makeshift community of fellow partiers who were happy to help him find ways for him to spend his money. It wouldn't be too speculative to assume that this son probably had a great time while he "squandered his inheritance in reckless living." The term "reckless living" suggests that the son partied his inheritance away. He probably drank, laughed, spent lots of money, had sex, and laughed some more with his friends.

There are at least two common reactions to this kind of lifestyle, and both are unfortunately way off course. The first reaction is to think this is really "living it up!" This perhaps is the most common reaction to a statement about lots of parties, money and sex. The mass majority would think this lifestyle is a sort of heaven on earth. Unfortunately, the result of seeking this lifestyle as a pursuit of true joy is like trying to gather an armful of wind. The season of joy may be there, but the promise of an enduring joy is a mirage.

The second reaction to a statement about someone living the hedonistic life is to think that seeking pleasure is altogether wrong. There's nothing wrong with pursuing pleasure, in fact Scripture is full of pursuing joy in Christ. It's what John Piper refers to as "Christian Hedonism."[3] The way in which we pursue pleasure is the issue, not pleasure itself. The practical application of the prodigal son's story is not "just say no" to pleasure. The practical message is seek pleasure in the things that will bring everlasting joy, not a fleeting spark.

Solomon, the author of Ecclesiastes, serves as a guinea pig on pursuing pleasure as means to true joy:

> I said in my heart, "Come now, I will test you with pleasure; enjoy yourself." But behold, this also was vanity. I said of laughter, "It is mad," and of pleasure, "What use is it?" I searched with my heart how to cheer my body with wine- my heart still guiding me with wisdom- and how to lay hold on folly, till I might see what was good for the children of man to do under heaven during the few days of their life.... I also gathered for myself silver and gold and the treasures of kings and provinces. I got singers, both men and women, and many concubines, the delight of the children of man (Ecclesiastes 2:1-3, 8).

Solomon tried laughter. He tried partying and alcohol. He tried spending large sums of money. He was "livin' la vida loca." He even tried lots of sex as a means to gain true joy. He had seven hundred wives and three hundred concubines (1 Kings 11:3). If he slept with a different one every night, once every three years he would be with the same woman. Here's his response to seeking pleasure as means to true joy:

> Then I considered all that my hands had done and the toil I had expended in doing it, and behold, all was vanity and a striving after wind, and there was nothing to be gained under the sun (Ecclesiastes 2:11).

Much like the prodigal son, Solomon's pursuit of joy down the road of "reckless living" proved to be pointless.

There's a song that we sometimes sing at church called "Satisfied." The lyrics to one of the verses remind me of the prodigal son's departure for true joy:

> Poor I was, and sought for riches,
> Something that would satisfy,
> But the dust I gathered round me
> Only mocked my soul's sad cry.[4]

The Good Life?

No doubt the son had a great time for a season, but the time came when "he had spent everything" and "a severe famine arose in that country, and he began to be in need" (Luke 15:14). The party ended.

He was in such need that he found a job feeding pigs and was so famished that he "was longing to be fed with the pods that the pigs ate, and no one gave him anything" (Luke 15:16).

He found out the hard way that "there was nothing to be gained under the sun" (Ecclesiastes 2:11) in that lifestyle. His money dried up, and when it did, so did his makeshift friends, the party, the sex and the laughter. Now his community would be these unclean animals whose food he coveted. Sin had taken him down a road that led to a place that he never wanted to be. The road was fun for a while, but in the end he found himself craving pig slop. Wisdom teaches us, "There is a way that seems right to a man, but its end is the way to death" (Proverbs 14:12).

The reality is that there are certain freedoms that are debilitating. To say it the opposite way, there are some restraints that provide some extraordinary freedoms. Two examples of this misconception of freedom come to mind from my experience with animals.

King

The first example was the time when my brother and I decided to liberate a local dog named King. From the backyard of the house where I used to live, we could see into the fenced-in area of our neighbor's yard. Our neighbors had a dog named King that looked to me as if he felt very constrained by the fenced-in area. One day, I talked to my older brother Travis about the oppression that the poor dog was experiencing, and as we spoke we realized that we were the ones who should set him free! Surely he would want to run wild and feel the breeze in his mangy hair and experience what the other undomesticated, unoppressed animals of the woods felt! It was the summer and the neighbors were away at work, so the timing was perfect. We walked down to their yard and opened the gate and yelled, "Run King! You're free! You were born for this! This is what life is all about boy!" I'm not sure we said all of that, but it was pretty dramatic for us. As we screamed at the dog to run for freedom, we realized that he wasn't entirely sure what to do with his newfound freedom. The best I can remember, he wandered around in the weeds close to their house. He didn't even run away very far.

When the owners arrived home that night they noticed the gate was open and King was missing. They started calling for him to return home. Travis and I knew where he was, and we were watching everything unfold. We went and got him from the weeds and took him back to our neighbors. They were so happy and thankful to us, and considered us to be quite the heroes. We, of course, never revealed that we were the ones who set the dog free. They even paid us for our good neighborly service. We tried to refuse, but in the end, what can you do?

Despite my obvious flaws of that day, I learned that it wasn't in King's best interest to have that kind of freedom. He didn't even know what to do with his freedom. He wandered around in the road and then got dirty in the weeds. What was best for him was the fence.

Jamboree

The other example from an animal comes from a much more recent experience. One day, some of my students skipped one of their classes and drove to Wal-Mart and purchased a fish for me. The reason they purchased the fish for me was because I mentioned something about wanting one. I didn't really expect them to get me a fish, much less, skip class and drive to Wal-Mart and buy me a fish that day. I was teaching another class when they walked into my room with the special delivery. I was shocked and speechless.

"What are you going to name him?" they asked.

"I can't believe you skipped class, drove to Wal-Mart and bought me a fish!" I replied.

"You said you wanted one!"

"I didn't say I wanted you to skip another class to get it!"

"Sorry, we didn't know…but what are you gonna name him?"

I looked at the fish and realized the great lengths to which my students had gone to get this special golden-colored beautiful fish, and I said, "His name is Jamboree." Applause erupted in the class over Jamboree, and for the rest of the day he sat in a bowl gleefully watching me work.

Students came by throughout the day and consistently asked two questions. The first was, "Where'd he come from?" My response was to mumble something they wouldn't understand so as to not get my students in trouble. The less people knew that they had skipped class, the better. The second question was, "What are you going to do with him?" My response to this question was, "I'm gonna leave him in the bowl and take care of him!"

As I repeated this phrase throughout the day, I realized that what was best for Jamboree was for him to remain in the bowl. It wouldn't be very freeing for him if I let him out of the water onto my desk to hang out for a while. His freedom was found within the boundaries of the bowl.

It seems that we struggle with this view of sin as being something that will be an expression of true freedom. "Christianity" may seem too restraining, but God has created us for His glory (Isaiah 43:7) and He knows that sin is not true freedom for us. He wants what's best for us, and like Jamboree and water, what's best for us is the context of His presence. As Tim Keller says, "You deliberately lose your freedom to engage in some things in order to release yourself to a richer kind of freedom to accomplish other things."[5]

Excursus On Consequences Of Sin

When I taught high school Bible classes at a Christian school, inevitably, when I would teach about some of the natural consequences of sin, I would receive an almost angry response from my students. For instance, when talking about marriage as the safe and God-glorifying context for sex, and the disobedience and dangers of sex outside of marriage, the reactions were at times hostile.

Mr. McMurray, "Are you suggesting that everyone who has sex outside of marriage will get an STD?" Or, "You think that looking at porn now means that I'll cheat on my wife later!?" Of course I never taught such things because they're simply not true, but the reaction to sin having consequences was twisted into these types of mangled questions.

While it's not true that every case leads to the same outcome, it is true that sin takes people farther than they want to go. Most, if not all "big sins" start with something "small." It doesn't mean that every person who goes and parties hard will end up eating pig food. It also doesn't mean that every person who has sex outside of marriage will get an STD, or even be unhappy for that matter. To say that there are consequences for sin is simply to say that whether seen or unseen, whether sooner or later, there are consequences for our disobedience to God. God is able to redeem and transform even our disobedience into situations that bring Him glory (Acts 2:23, 4:27-28), but this still doesn't change the reality that there are consequences for sin (see Hebrews 10:30-31; John 8:34; Romans 6:23; Psalm 38:1-11; Isaiah 59:2; Ephesians 4:18; Ephesians 2:1, 5; Titus 3:3).

I draw attention to this issue only to point out that when the prodigal son hits hard times, it is an undeniable natural consequence to his rebellious living. Whether we want to admit it or not, sin has led him to a place that he never wanted to be. As Thomas Watson said, "Sin first courts, and then kills."[6]

Conclusion

The son "came to himself" (Luke 15:17) and realized how good his father was to even the servants. He decided it would be best to return home. He even prepared a speech for his father not knowing how he would respond. The next chapter will explore the response of the father.

The son went far away from the father in this story. It is true for many of us as well that we wander away from God. At times, we have distanced ourselves from the benevolence of our loving Father. We have chosen to go our own way and do our own thing. It is in the context of this distance that the length of God's love is magnified. No matter what you have done or how far you have strayed; you are never beyond the reach of God's love!

2

How Far His Reach

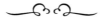

"And he arose and came to his father. But while he was still a long way off, his father saw him and felt compassion, and ran and embraced him and kissed him. And the son said to him, 'Father, I have sinned against heaven and before you. I am no longer worthy to be called your son.' But the father said to his servants, 'Bring quickly the best robe, and put it on him, and put a ring on his hand, and shoes on his feet. And bring the fattened calf and kill it, and let us eat and celebrate. For this my son was dead, and is alive again; he was lost and is found.' And they began to celebrate." –Luke 15:20-24

Watching

My two-year old son loves trains. That may be an understatement. He thinks about them, talks about them, plays with them, looks for them... it's a constant fascination for him. As a matter of fact, while I'm writing this, he and Jennifer are in a little town called Belmont close to where we live on a "train hunt." It was his reward for a job well done with potty-training this week. Belmont has a train track that runs right through the middle of it, and several times throughout the day, the train will come through blowing its whistle. There's a park right beside the tracks, and we'll go and play in the park waiting and watching for the train to come. The anticipation of a train coming is visible in my son. You can see it in his eyes. Any glimmer of hope of hearing a distant blow of the whistle, he perks up and says "A train! A train!" and then we run across the park to get a better view.

This is the image that comes to mind when I read the story of the prodigal son's father watching for his son to come: "But while he was still a long way off, his father saw him" (Luke 15:20). There is a sense of anticipation. He has been watching the horizons for the outline of his boy to top the distant hills. And when he sees him, he must have shouted, "My son! My son!"

It's hard to hold back tears when you read this and realize that you're the son in this story. All the times (years for me) of trying to ignore God and trying to get distance from Him, and not giving a thought about Him are reciprocated with a Father who hasn't forgotten the son. More than not forgetting, the father is looking for him. Henri Nouwen writes: "God is looking into the distance for me, trying to find me, and longing to bring me home…He is the One who is looking for me while I am doing the hiding."[1]

"With Suffering"

Jennifer and I got home one day to see the answering machine blinking, informing us that someone had called and left us a message. I pushed the button and we both listened. As soon as we heard what was said, we looked at each other and smiled and pushed the button again. Here's what it said:

Compassion. It means 'with suffering.' 'Passion' means 'suffering' and the prefix 'com' means 'with.' Compassion…with suffering. Isn't that beautiful? This is Buddy, hope you all are doing well. I just wanted to call and share that with you. Think about that today. Click.

That was it, short and simple and to the point. Maybe you get those kinds of phone messages a lot, but Jennifer and I don't, and so we replayed it to make sure we heard it correctly. We not only thought about it that day, but I've remembered it clearly ever since. I would say that was a pretty effective phone message.

The word compassion is used to describe what the father felt for his son in Luke 15:20. "His father saw him and felt compassion." The Greek word basically means to feel a yearning within the gut. It's a yearning that one would feel with suffering.

This is the kind of compassion that God displays for His children when they return home no matter what they've done. Romans 2:4 says, "God's kindness is meant to lead you to repentance." The son is coming home with a prepared speech about becoming a servant to the father, while the father is looking at the son with compassion. His boy is not a servant, and he doesn't have to earn his love.

Lightning Bolt

I love the Olympics. For two solid weeks, Jennifer and I would sit down at night and watch incredible athletes compete in fascinating sports. My friend Jake makes fun of people like me for getting all worked up about the Olympics asking questions like, "Am I supposed to be fired up about people bouncing on trampolines?" While I understand his point, I'm still enthralled by the whole production, and I'm not alone. One night, several people, including Jake, went to our pastor's house for dinner, and at some point in the conversation, I hear my pastor say, "Badminton is amazing!" Jake puts his fork down, elbows me, looks straight into my face and repeats what he had just heard, "Badminton is amazing," stating it in a tone that suggested that he had just provided ample evidence of the fact that the Olympic craze had gotten out of hand.

I certainly haven't kept up with most of those sports since then, but it was thrilling to watch at the time. While the swimming events were arguably the most exciting in Beijing, my favorite event in the Olympics is the one hundred meter run, and in 2008, it was a memorable one. The favorite going into the race was a guy named Usain Bolt from Jamaica. As with most of the athletes in the other events, I had never heard of him. After watching him run that night, I'll never forget him. The one hundred meter race is extremely short. It's over in ten seconds. When the gun sounded for the runners to begin, they all jumped off to a good start. Midway through the race, Bolt pulled ahead, and with about fifteen meters remaining, he had such a lead that he began to celebrate the victory. He not only won the gold medal, but also broke the world record. Very likely, it is the fastest a human being has ever run.

When I read the story of the prodigal son's father, I'm struck with this image of him running to his son. The way Jesus tells the story, it's easy to imagine that the father takes off when he sees his son! I don't get a visual of a slow steady jog with the father taking breaks along the way to put his hands on his knees. The visual I see is one of the father taking off in a sprint to meet his son on the horizon.

If you've ever run to meet someone, then you know the intensity of the emotions that put those feet into action. If you've ever had someone run to meet you, then you know the sweetness of having someone care for you so much that his or her legs must move quicker than usual. When I pick my son up from nursery at church, he'll spot me from across the room and drop what he's doing and run like Usain Bolt to get to me. The excitement simply will not allow his legs to walk at a slow normal pace.

This is a visual of God's excited love for us. As John Piper says, "Well-to-do, dignified, aristocratic, aging men don't run, they walk. They keep their composure. They show that they are on top of their emotions. But not in Jesus' story about God's joy over His people."[2] He not only watches for us, and feels compassion for us, He also runs to welcome us home!

Not The Time For A Handshake

Airports are amazing to me. People are either coming or going, or they're there to see others who are coming or going. It's really a pretty emotional place. I remember going to the airport several years ago when my good friends bought a one-way ticket to Jerusalem because they were moving there. I hugged Alex and Jaime and we said our goodbyes. At the same time, there were probably other people in the same airport welcoming home someone they loved with a giant hug. These kinds of goodbyes and arrivals require more than a handshake. The outward act of a hug requires little movement, but a greater, unseen inward movement of affection usually accompanies it.

My friend Nathan says studies have shown that on average a person needs sixteen hugs a day to be a healthy individual. I'm not sure if he made that up or not, but either way, I think he's on to something. There's something about a hug that has a way of breaking down barriers. It's easier to feel comfortable with someone when they greet you with a warm hug than it is with a cold handshake. I know some people really value personal space, but I'd much rather be greeted with a hug.

In the context of the story of the prodigal son, the embrace of the father and son is quite moving. The last time they had seen each other, there was probably no hug. The son had told the father that he basically wished he would hurry up and die, because he wanted his inheritance. The father gave the son his portion of it, and the son left. This was their last time together.

The son was expecting an awkward reunion with his father, one of pleading to be hired as a servant. He didn't know how his father would react to his return. He knew he was good and benevolent, as seen by his remembrance of his father: "How many of my father's hired servants have more than enough bread..." (Luke 15:17). But while he knew his father was good and benevolent, he apparently wasn't expecting this sweet of a reunion. This is how Jesus describes the scene: "While he was still a long way off, his father saw him and felt compassion, and ran and embraced him and kissed him" (Luke 15:20). What was said before had been forgiven. The smell of pigs was ignored in the embrace of his father. And while there was much more outward movement in the previous scene of the father running to meet the son, there is more inward motion in this scene of being together again. This is what the father had wanted, the return of his lost son.

Rembrandt painted a picture about this particular scene. The son is on his knees, and the father is hugging his boy. It's a beautiful image depicting the love described in Jesus' story. The son looks worn out in his ragged clothes, but the yellows and browns of his rags look beautiful in the context of the painting. Henri Nouwen made this observation about the painting: "In the context of a compassionate embrace, our brokenness may appear beautiful, but our brokenness has no other beauty but the beauty that comes from the compassion that surrounds it."[3]

Best Robe!

I love my group of friends. When Jennifer and I first moved to this area, one of the things that we prayed for consistently was for good community. God was so faithful to us in the way that he answered our prayers. Every week, our group gets together to bowl or play flag football, or disc golf, or play games, etc. Over the past couple of years, we've started describing things that are pleasing to us with the accolade of calling it the "best." For instance, recently I asked one of my friends if a restaurant's grilled cheese was any good. His response was a very predictable: "Best grilled cheese." It's pretty ridiculous actually. I've been accused of speaking in exaggerations, but this is extreme. Often, it makes very little sense, and I'm starting to wonder if we really know what the word "best" means. It's a comparative term that means that something surpasses all others in excellence. So when someone says something like, "the sun feels great today," a response of "best sun," doesn't make much sense. In my limited knowledge of things in outer space, I believe there's only one sun, so I'm not sure what other suns it's being compared to. Either way, now I'm guilty of doing the same thing.

This past winter several churches in our area decided to plan a student ski trip together. As we discussed the name and theme, we of course came up with "Best Ski Trip." We had hoodies made and everything. It actually turned out truly to be the best ski trip.

Maybe it's because of my friends that what the father says to the servants sticks out to me so much in this story: "The father said to his servants, 'Bring quickly the best robe, and put it on him, and put a ring on his hand, and shoes on his feet" (Luke 15:22).

Not just any robe would do. It had to be the "Best Robe." His father wanted to get him a robe that surpassed all others in excellence. He wanted to replace the old with something new that signified his sonship! The son had tried to give his speech about being "no longer worthy to be called a son" (Luke 15:21), but the father interrupts him with his eagerness to restore him and make things new. He tells the servants to hurry up and get his son the best they can find. It's an astonishing picture of Christ's eagerness to restore us into relationship with Him. "Therefore, if anyone is in Christ, he is a new creation. The old has passed away; behold, the new has come" (2 Corinthians 5:17).

The imagery of the best robe reminds me of the last verse in the hymn, "The Solid Rock." The latter part of the verse says, "Dressed in His righteousness alone, faultless to stand before the throne!"[4] The father's eager display of clothing his son in a new wardrobe is a picture of God's eager display of love toward us.

A Chubby Little Cow For A Great Big Party

My wife Jennifer used to work for an organization called YoungLife. It's a ministry that focuses on building relationships with high school students with the goal of showing them the love of Christ and sharing with them the Gospel. Jennifer's first day on the job was to go to a camp in Colorado with students she didn't even know. Where I would've been a complete disaster, she's incredibly gifted at building relationships quickly. We both knew that the week would be great and that the students going would hear the Gospel clearly presented. Before she left I made her a little art project centered on the theme of celebrating what God would do.

I'm one of the least artistic people I know, but I love the idea of art, and so I attempted to make a miniature table. I found some little scrap pieces of wood, nailed some legs onto it, and then painted it. It wasn't beautiful, but it would work. Jennifer's brother Matthew gave me a little stuffed cow he received from Chick-fil-A® in some kind of give away. I took the cow and strapped it to the table and painted this statement underneath it:

> "'Bring the fattened calf and kill it, and let us eat and celebrate. For this my son was dead, and is alive again; he was lost and is found.' And they began to celebrate" (Luke 15:23-24). Celebrating those who will come to Christ this week at camp!

When Jennifer returned from camp, she told us about the students who stood up and accepted Christ that week, and we thanked God in celebration for what He had done.

When the son came back home, his father threw him a party. Not only did he watch for his son, show compassion to him, run to meet him, embrace him, give him the best robe, a ring, and new shoes, but he also has the fattest little calf he owned killed for the biggest party he could throw. It was the "best calf" for the "best party."

The Other Lost Son

Not all of the reactions were joyful to the son's return. The older son was so mad that he didn't even attend the party. His father goes to him and explains, "you are always with me, and all that is mine is yours. It was fitting to celebrate and be glad, for this your brother was dead, and is alive; he was lost, and is found" (Luke 15:31-32).

The picture of the older brother illustrates the Pharisees' reaction to Jesus receiving and eating with sinners (Luke 15:2). Like the older brother, the Pharisees had a hard time understanding the grace of the father. Like the older brother, the Pharisees had been guilty of thinking that the father's love was something to be earned. Like the older brother, the Pharisees missed the celebration of the dead brought back to life and the lost found.

Conclusion

The story of the prodigal son shows the far-reaching love of Christ. No matter how far away we've run, His arm reaches farther. As God says in Isaiah 50:2, "Is My hand shortened, that it cannot redeem?" and again in Isaiah 59:1, "Behold, the Lord's hand is not shortened, that it cannot save." Nehemiah 1:9 says, "Though your dispersed be under the farthest skies, I will gather them from there and bring them to the place that I have chosen." No matter how far you've gone, you are within the reach of His love! As my friends would say, this is Best News. God is a God of grace!

Father, we pray that according to the riches of Your glory, that we would have the strength to comprehend that the length of Your love is beyond all measure (Ephesians 3:14-19).

Response:

"Jesus! What a Friend for sinners!
Jesus! Lover of my soul;
Friends may fail me, foes assail me,
He, my Savior, makes me whole.

Hallelujah! What a Savior!
Hallelujah! What a Friend!
Saving, helping, keeping, loving,
He is with me to the end.

Jesus! I do now adore Him,
More than all in Him I find.
He hath granted me forgiveness,
I am His, and He is mine.

Hallelujah! What a Savior!
Hallelujah! What a Friend!
Saving, helping, keeping, loving,
He is with me to the end."[5]

Part 2

Widespread

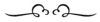

3

How Widespread the Condition

"And a leper came to Him, imploring Him, and kneeling said to Him, 'If you will, you can make me clean.'" –Mark 1:40

The goal of this chapter and the next is to look at the breadth of Christ's love for us, with the hope that we see that no one is outside the boundaries of His love. No matter who a person is, what their history is, where they grew up, or how much of an outcast they are, Christ's love reaches to the furthest bounds. There is no individual or people group that is beyond the reach of the comprehensive nature of His love. It is a vast canopy that covers all, and as His love is comprehensive, so too is our sin comprehensive. The Puritan author Ralph Venning once said, "As God is holy, all holy, only holy, altogether holy, and always holy, and so sin is sinful, all sinful, only sinful, altogether sinful, and always sinful."[1] In order to understand the breadth of the cure, we must first understand the breadth of the condition. In other words, before we care that there is a remedy for our sickness, we must understand that we are sick.

A Widespread Sickness

The whole world is suffering from the effects of the fall of man. Sin has reached to the furthest bounds; there is no place on earth where its hand is not seen. Creation itself is currently in "bondage" (Romans 8:20), and "the whole creation has been groaning together in the pains of childbirth" (Romans 8:22). Sin is widespread in the way that it has affected the world, and in the way that it affects every individual. In truth, every part of every individual is infected by sin. It is a pervasive cancer in each person.

In Mark 1:40, a leper approaches Jesus. Leprosy is a horrible disease that affects every part of a person. It is a comprehensive sickness, and in biblical days no cure was known. The disease has great breadth to the way that it reduces a human into something that scarcely resembles a human. The condition is torturous in its disfiguration of a person: discolored patches on the skin, sores that emit foul discharge, bleaching and loss of hair (including eye lashes and eye brows), sores on the throat that cause a hoarse sounding voice, loss of fingers and toes, and ulcerating hands and feet. This continues to eat away at a person for years, and often decades. The nerves begin to decay and then there is a loss of feeling, resulting in parts of the body rotting away.[2]

On top of the physical suffering is the social suffering of having leprosy. The Levitical law stated, "And the leper in whom the plague is, his clothes shall be rent, and his head bare, and he shall put a covering upon his upper lip, and shall cry, 'Unclean, unclean,' all the days wherein the plague shall be in him, he shall be defiled; he is unclean: he shall dwell alone; without the camp shall be his habitation" (Leviticus 13:45-46). The clothes were ripped, the head was shaved, and the covering was placed over this hideous disease. However, the covering only covered up the ugliness of the disease; it certainly didn't hide the fact that a person was a leper. There was no hiding it. If it wasn't seen clearly from the way the infected person was covered, there was the added social humiliation of being required to cry aloud, "Unclean! Unclean!" Imagine the embarrassment of walking around and screaming that you were unclean. You walk into Wal-Mart yelling, "Unclean, Unclean!" Imagine the disgusting looks you would get. There was no hiding the condition of leprosy. The sight, sound and smell would quickly give away your deplorable and hopeless condition.

Leprosy is a poignant picture of sin. Most of us wouldn't want to see our sin like leprosy, but it is a remarkable parallel to our condition. Leprosy runs deep. Leprosy defiles a person. Leprosy isolates a person from community. Leprosy spreads from one part to another part. Leprosy causes a person to be unclean. Sin is comparable in each way: it's deep, it defiles, it isolates, it spreads, and it makes us unclean. As the prophet Isaiah says, "We have all become like one who is unclean, and all our righteous deeds are like a polluted garment" (Is. 64:6). Sin has made us filthy and polluted.

J.C. Ryle stated of leprosy, "It is a radical disease of the whole man. Just like sin, it attacks not merely the skin, but the blood, the flesh and bones, until the unhappy patient begins to lose its extremities, and to rot by inches."[3] Like leprosy, sin is malignant. Jerry Bridges writes of malignancy, "Medically, the word malignant describes a tumor of potentially unlimited growth that expands locally into adjoining tissue by invasion and systemically by metastasizing into other areas of the body."[4] The picture of sin is clear, and as leprosy covered the entirety of a man, so too does sin.

The totality of sickness is what theologians sometimes refer to as "total depravity." It means that "sin as a universal deformity of human nature, is found at every point in every person (1 Kings 8:46; Rom. 3:9-23; 7:18; 1 John 1:8-10)."[5] It doesn't mean that people are as bad as they possibly could be; it just refers to the idea that sin is extensively found throughout each individual. The whole person is corrupt. In this way, sin is much like leprosy. Like the leper, the corruption may not be as bad as it could possibly be, but it is corrupting each part of the person. Sin is comprehensive, and it is a destroyer. The Westminster Confession states,

Man by his fall into a state of sin, hast wholly lost all ability of will to any spiritual good accompanying salvation; so as a natural man, being altogether averse from that good, and dead in sin, is not able by his own strength to convert himself, or to prepare himself thereunto.[6]

In other words, there is no cure found from within. If there is a hope for our condition, then this hope must be found from outside of ourselves, for we are not able by our own strength to convert ourselves. Like the leper, hope was to be found outside of his own ability and strength, so too, our hope is not from our own ability or strength.

It was from this condition that the man approaches Jesus and says, "If you will, you can make me clean" (Mark 1:40). Luke's gospel tells us that he was "covered with leprosy" (Luke 5:12). It had probably been years since he had been touched or looked at with a smile. His statement is simple and brimming with a mixture of faith and doubt. This spotted outcast approaches the spotless Christ and simply says, "If you want to, you can fix me." You can hear the inflated feeling of hope. It is a faith-filled statement of Christ's ability, but mixed with a doubtful tone concerning His willingness. There are many who may feel the same way, "I know Christ could cleanse me, but would He really want to?"

Here was a man who was literally decaying both inside and out with leprosy. There was no community for him. There were no close friends. There was no human touch.

One of my favorite things to do in the world is to laugh. I love people with a good sense of humor. I'm not really much for jokes, but good wit in well-timed situations is extremely enjoyable to me. Sometimes, it's actually true that laughter is the best medicine. The thing about laughter, at least for me, is that I rarely sit around and laugh by myself. I laugh with friends in community. I laugh with my family. One of the saddest aspects of this story, as I try to imagine this man, is the lack of laughter. He probably lived in a leper colony, which means he would have had somewhat of a community, but I can't imagine that laughter was the sound bouncing off the cave walls. Death was a very present reality for a leper colony, and death and laughter aren't well-acquainted companions. I imagine this man with little joy and a glaring absence of any kind of avenue by which to express any glimmer of joy he may have had. This was his condition.

The message of this Scripture gives hope that there is no person outside the breadth of Christ's love. No matter who we are or how unclean we may be, Christ's love comes to us in our condition. Aren't we like the leper? Isn't this our condition? Love is shown, but not because of our beauty. In fact, love is shown in spite of our obvious lack of beauty.

Three Sick People From Dr. Luke's Gospel

One of the writers of Scripture was a doctor named Luke. In Colossians 4:14 Paul says, "Luke the beloved physician greets you." If Paul hadn't told us his profession, we could probably tell by his writing style. He writes about medical conditions with medical terms. Those of us who aren't doctors don't typically toss medical terminology around in our every day conversations. When you read Luke's writings, it sometimes feels like you're seeing through a doctor's lens. He writes about the "woman with an issue of blood" (Luke 8:43), about Jesus' circumcision (Luke 2:21), about feet and ankle bones (Acts 3:8), and so it's not surprising to see Luke write about sick people. Beyond writing about medical conditions, he has a way of describing people throughout his gospel that pushes the medical imagery to the forefront of our minds, even when the narrative has nothing to do with the medical. In what follows, we'll consider three 'patients' from his gospel, although none are actually physically sick.

By looking at these three examples from Luke's Gospel, we'll see that Jesus loves the unlovable, the unwanted, the rejected, the broken, the downcast, and the outcast...we'll ultimately see that there is no one outside the bounds of His love.

Matthew, The Tax Collector

The first patient is Matthew, the tax collector. Jesus comes to him in Luke 5:27 saying, "Follow

Me." Tax collectors were a hated group. They were considered cheats and thieves. When Jesus calls Matthew, he leaves everything and follows Him. He then throws a party and invites Jesus and his friends. The Pharisees grumble about Jesus going to this party with filthy sinners. They were shocked that He would associate with this riff-raff. Jesus responded to the religious healthy, "Those who are well have no need of a physician, but those who are sick. I have not come to call the righteous but sinners to repentance" (Luke 5:31-32).

I hate going to the doctor. I hate the whole process, and I hate what it reveals about me. A couple of years ago, I realized that great pride was being exposed in my lack of desire to go to the doctor. It came to my realization that there were two reasons why I didn't like going to the doctor. I either felt that I wasn't that sick, or that I could fix my sickness on my own, both of which are rooted in pride.

There have been numerous occasions in which I was sick, but felt that I wasn't sick enough to go to the doctor. I go into this bizarre denial of sickness in order to stay away from the infirmary. The problem with this is that it's extremely dangerous to be sick and not realize it. It's like getting shot in the chest and putting a band-aid on it.

Spiritually, we must understand that we are sick. Jesus came for the sick, not for the healthy. Pride is what keeps one from seeing his own spiritual sickness. What qualifies us as being one for whom Christ came is sickness!

The other reason I don't like to go see doctors is that I sometimes don't think they can do anything to help me. As I write this, I realize this is an embarrassing display of pride; but it's true. In other words, I realize that I'm sick, I just don't trust that there's much they can do to help.

I've counseled several people over the years with this view of Christ. They don't need convinced that they're spiritually sick. The problem of sin is easily recognized in their lives, they just don't believe that Christ can really fix them. The problem with this is that the Jesus of the Gospels speaks directly to the unworthy, not the righteous. There is no one too unclean or too sick for Him. In fact, He came for the unclean and sick! The example of how Jesus relates to people is instructive for us. Matthew was a traitor to the Jewish people. He was a social outcast. People didn't want to hang out with tax collectors, yet Jesus loved the unwanted.

The Woman Who Was A Sinner

The second patient is a woman found in Luke 7:37-38:

And behold, a woman of the city, who was a sinner, when she learned that He was reclining at table in the Pharisee's house, brought an alabaster flask of ointment, and standing behind Him at His feet, weeping, she began to wet His feet with her tears and wiped them

with the hair of her head and kissed His feet
and anointed them with the ointment.

The woman in this text is described as "a great
sinner." She came to this dinner party uninvited and
unannounced simply to see Jesus. She's not noble or
godly. There were others present at dinner certainly
more impressive morally than this woman. But Jesus
is a friend of sinners, and His grace is magnified in
the object of His love.

Simon, the Pharisee who had invited Jesus over
to dinner, was disturbed by the display of the woman
and the fact that Jesus didn't rebuke her. Jesus then
tells Simon a parable about a moneylender who had
two debtors. One owed ten times more than the other,
however, the moneylender cancelled the debt of both
men. Jesus asks Simon, "Now which of them will love
him more?" (Luke 7:42). Simon responds correctly
by saying that the one who had the larger debt would
love him more. Jesus then uses the example of the
woman and concludes, "Her sins, which are many,
are forgiven- for she loved much. But he who is
forgiven little, loves little" (Luke 7:47). When the
weight of sin is recognized, there is corresponding
recognition of the weight of His love.

Some may think that this means the more they
sin, the more Christ loves them, but this is not what
is meant. What is meant is that an awareness of our
condition and what we've been saved from, leads to a
greater love for the One who saved us. Ray Comfort
illustrates this truth in a sermon,

You see, if you came to me and said, "Hey, Ray," and I said, "Yeah." You said, "This is a cure to Groaninzin's disease; I sold my house to raise the money to get this cure. I'm giving it to you as a free gift." I'd probably react something like this: "What? Cure to what? Groaninzin's disease? You sold your house to raise the money to get this cure? You're giving it to me as a free gift? Why, thanks a lot. Bye...That guy's a nut." I mean, that's probably how I'd react if you sold your house to raise the money to get a cure for a disease I'd never heard of and your giving it to me as free gift, I'd think you're rather strange.

But instead, if you came to me and said, "Ray, you've got Groaninzin's disease. I can see ten clear symptoms on your flesh. You're going to be dead in two weeks." And I became convinced I had the disease (the symptoms were so evident), and said, "Oh! What shall I do?" And then you said, "Don't worry. This is a cure to Groaninzin's disease. I sold my house to raise the money to get this cure. I'm giving it to you as a free gift." I'm not going to despise your sacrifice; I'm going to appreciate it and I'm going to appropriate it. Why? Because I've seen the disease that I might appreciate the cure.[7]

It is by recognizing our condition that we rejoice that we've been saved from it. The issue is not that the one who piles up sins will be forgiven more than the one who is squeaky clean. The issue is that those who think they are squeaky clean don't recognize their true condition, and thus don't recognize the beauty of being rescued from it. Jesus says it this way: "Those who are well have no need of a physician, but those who are sick. I have not come to call the righteous but sinners to repentance" (Luke 5:31-32).

The way Jesus relates to this unnamed woman described only as "a sinner" shows how Christ came to "seek and save the lost" (Luke 19:10). He was and is a friend to sinners, and as Matthew, the tax collector, showed us how Jesus loved the unwanted, this woman shows us how Jesus loved the sinful.

The Tax Collector

The third patient is an unnamed tax collector found in Luke 18. This passage is the contrasting story of two prayers from two men. One stands and prays, "God, I thank you that I am not like other men, extortioners, unjust, adulterers, or even like this tax collector. I fast twice a week; I give tithes of all that I get" (vv. 11-12). The other, "would not even lift up his eyes to heaven, but beat his breast, saying, 'God, be merciful to me, a sinner!'" (v. 13). Jesus' response to the picture of these two men is that the latter "went down to his house justified" (v. 14), while the other did not.

Jesus was not interested in the morality of the Pharisee or his religious expressions. He was guilty of judging his righteousness by comparing himself to others. He didn't recognize his own condition.

Scripture says that "all our righteous deeds are like a polluted garment" (Isaiah 64:6); hardly anything to stand up and brag about. The end result for this Pharisee is that he goes home moral, religious, comparatively clean, but unjustified before God.

The tax collector however, recognized the weight of his sinful condition. He didn't brag about tithing or fasting or anything else. He simply said, "God, be merciful to me, a sinner!" The end result for this immoral sinner was that "he went home justified" (v. 14).

The purpose of the story of this tax collector is to show that God is not impressed with those who feel no need for Him. Those who recognize their sickness, and cry out to Him for help, are the ones that bring Him glory. Jesus loved the unwanted. He loved the sinful. And He loved the broken.

Conclusion

The only prerequisite for Christ's healing love is to be sick and recognize it. This is the story of the leper, Matthew, the sinful woman, and the unnamed tax collector. Their sinful condition was widespread. It was not hidden. It was clearly seen and observed by others. These are sweet words for those who realize the broad-sweeping malignancy of the sin within their lives. There is hope!

4

How Widespread the Cure

*"Moved with pity, He stretched out His hand
and touched him and said to him, "I will;
be clean." And immediately the leprosy left
him, and he was made clean. And Jesus
sternly charged him and sent him away at
once, and said to him, "See that you say
nothing to anyone, but go, show yourself to
the priest and offer for your cleansing what
Moses commanded, for a proof to them."
But he went out and began to talk freely
about it, and to spread the news, so that
Jesus could no longer openly enter a town,
but was out in desolate places, and people
were coming to him from every quarter."
–Mark 1:41-45*

"Wash me, and I will be whiter than snow."
–Psalm 51:7

A Remedy For My Sickness

A couple of months ago, I went to a camp with the youth from our church. While at camp, I lost my voice and developed a hacking cough. My chest felt terrible; it felt like my lungs were filling with liquid. The physical aspect was not fun at all, but I really hated the social hindrances. I had no desire to start a conversation due to the fact that I couldn't maneuver through it without my voice giving up on me. The problem came when people would ask me a question, and I had to quickly make the decision between trying to get vocal strength behind my answer or just whisper an answer. Both are equally awkward, but if the vocal part comes through, sometimes, people don't notice as much. If you whisper to someone then clearly it's awkward. Early on in the week I tried to hide the loss of my voice by responding to questions with vocal strength. After cracking a few times in prepubescent clumsiness, I decided the whisper approach would be less humiliating.

My sweet wife, watching everything unfold, realized that I was sick and that I needed to go to the doctor. In my pride, however, I decided that the doctor wouldn't really be able to do anything for me. I was apparently a special case that would blow the doctor's mind and he would feel so baffled that I would be sent away in the same condition.

As God's providence would have it, however, one of my students somehow lodged a stick, which was similar to the size of a small log into her toe, the one that the nursery rhyme refers to as the "little piggy that received no roast beef." There was no getting this particular splinter out, although several of the boy scouts in our youth group were quite willing to dig in. I had to take her to the doctor. There was another girl in our youth group who wants to study nursing in college, so I thought it wise to have her accompany the trip.

The three of us got to the local urgent care, and when I went to the window I did my best to describe the situation as my voice stumbled in and out of words. The lady looked at me and said, "sounds like somebody else needs to see the doctor too."

"No, I'm, *cough, cough, hack, hack*, I'm fine."

She rolled her eyes and went back to her paper work. I realized at this point that my wife was right the whole time, and so I pushed my insurance card through the window and asked to see the doctor as well.

The three of us: Molly, the girl with the splinter that wanted to kill the piggy that didn't get any roast beef; Sarah, the girl who loves medical stuff; and I, who hate the doctor, went back to watch the surgery unfold. The doctor numbed Molly's toe, and Molly watched our faces watch the toe being dismantled. My face had the look of horror... one of, "How does she not feel that?" Sarah, the future nurse, had a giddy, excited look as if she was opening a Christmas present. I kept watching as the doctor beat the fire out of her toe with tweezers until another doctor poked his head in and asked to see me.

After listening to the explanation of my condition and running a few little tests, the doctor diagnosed me with bronchitis. He filled out a prescription and sent me on my way. The other doctor finally got what looked to be a small conifer tree out of Molly's toe, and we were sent on our way. As we went back to camp with our medicines for pain and bronchitis, I realized that I was going to get better. Sure enough, the sickness went away pretty quickly. I learned some valuable lessons that weekend. First, my wife is almost always right. Second, if I am sick, I need a doctor, and the sooner the better.

The same idea applies to us spiritually. We are all sick and the sooner we realize it, the closer we are to the remedy. We need a doctor. The reality is that we have a sickness that is pervasive, but there is a cure that is even more comprehensive! Daniel Fuller uses the doctor analogy to depict this reality; "We must entrust our sick selves to Christ as the Great Physician, with confidence that He will work until our hellishness is transformed into godliness."[1]

A Remedy For The Leper

In the story of the leprous man, when Jesus sees and hears him in his condition, He is moved with compassion. It's actually weightier than what our word compassion denotes. It really means that when He saw the leprous man, He felt compassion in His gut for him. It makes me wonder if we look at people

74

with that kind of compassion, or if we mostly just look at people on a surface level. We quickly make our judgments about what kind of people they may or may not be, and how little we want to do with them. Jesus doesn't look at the guy with a disgusted look; rather he looks at him with a deep compassion. He came "that they may have life and have it abundantly" (John 10:10), and here was a man before Him whose life was taken away from him by a disease that covered the entire breadth of who he was.

Had Jesus looked at him with compassion and then healed him simply by speaking words, the story would still be remarkable. The short phrase at the end of verse 41 says, "He stretched out His hand and touched him," which adds another astonishing element to the nature of this story. No one talked to a leper, much less stood close to one, and certainly they would never touch one. By touching a leper, a person would be considered unclean as well. Jesus didn't have to touch him. We know from other stories in Scripture that Jesus doesn't even have to be in the same town as someone and still He is able to speak a word and bring healing (John 4:46-54).

In this story, Jesus is so moved with compassion, that He reaches out and touches the man with leprosy. The text literally reads, "He took hold of him." In other words, this wasn't a quick touch of the finger quickly jerked back, this was a touch that lingered, associated with, and expressed true compassion for the man. His disciples must have been freaking out over this. They must have assumed that their teacher would now contract this deadly disease! Jesus doesn't worry about the uncleanness or the reactions; He wasn't "afraid to touch and get involved."[2] He simply reaches out and touches the man in his condition. Had others touched the man, they would have been contaminated with the disease, but Christ in His purity touches and doesn't get dirty. He purifies!

Throughout the Gospels, we see that Jesus shows great compassion for people. He showed mercy to the blind beggar (Luke 18:38, 42), to ten lepers (Luke 17:13-14), to the naked demon-guy (Mark 5:19), and to the mother whose daughter was demon-possessed (Matthew 15:22). He showed compassion for a widow who had lost her son (Luke 7:13), and He showed pity to the father whose son was demon-possessed (Mark 9:22). He showed compassion for the hungry crowd (Mark 8:2), and for those who were like sheep without a shepherd (Mark 6:34). Truly, "The Lord is full of compassion and is merciful" (James 5:11). When He looks upon us in our condition, He sees us with unyielding compassion!

When I was a teacher at a Christian school, it was really an amazing job. I taught the Bible classes to high school guys. Imagine, if you dare, twenty-five to thirty high school guys without the accountability of ladies to help them act sane. There was never boredom in our classes. I was never much for locking my office door since I usually had my hands full with books and papers. This unfortunately, led to my office being used as somewhat of a community closet. I would come in sometimes and look around and notice things on my desk that had not been there before, and sometimes I wasn't entirely sure what those things were. One time I came to my office and a giant moth had been taped to my door, as if a cat had dropped it off for its proud owner or something. Another time, as I walked in, I noticed that all of my office items (i.e. stapler, phone, note pads, computer keyboard, etc...) were made into sandwiches. Each item was given a bun on the bottom and a bun on the top. There were never explanations, just random expressions of, "Hey, we've been here..." So, there were times when I would come in and look at something and give it a little nudge, but remove my fingers as quickly as possible to see if there was any way to figure out what the mysterious substance was. At other times, there would be Krispy Kreme doughnuts on my desk. On such occasions, I would "lay hold" of them. There is a huge difference between those types of touches. Jesus didn't barely touch the guy, He grabbed hold of the guy in compassion.

Homeless Louis

A friend of mine recently told me a story about a homeless man who had been coming to his church. He's affectionately called "Homeless Louis." Homeless Louis started coming to church because people in the church talked to him and seemed genuinely interested in him. He told my friend that he had lived in the country for six years, and no one had even cared what his name was until the people at the church spoke to him. The leprous man must have felt this way when Jesus reached out and touched him. He must have been overwhelmed by the fact that for years, people hadn't spoken with him or touched him, and then Jesus does both.

The man's short statement to Jesus was: "If you will, you can make me clean..." (v. 40). To this statement Jesus replies, "I will, be clean" (v. 41). The man's statement is like saying, "I know you are able to do it, it just depends on whether you want to or not." Jesus responds to this mixture of faith and doubt with beautiful simplicity, "I want to. Be clean!" This combination of His willingness and His ability shows the beauty of the Gospel. We have a God who is not only able to fix our sin problem, but He is willing to fix it. The incarnation of Christ teaches us this same truth. The God, who is able, shows His willingness to associate with us by entering into our world: "And the Word became flesh and dwelt among us" (John 1:14).

"Immediately the leprosy left him, and he was made clean" (v. 42). The condition of the man wasn't beyond the healing ability of Jesus. This gives such hope to us, that there are none who are beyond the breadth of His love. There is no condition that is too gross for His touch. He touches the leper and the leper becomes clean, but Jesus doesn't get dirty. There are a lot of people who feel like they're too dirty for Christ to bother with, but the Gospels reveal a different Jesus. The Jesus of the Gospels reaches out and touches those who are outcast and dirty. He isn't surprised by the condition; rather He shows compassion for those who suffer under hard conditions. The leprosy immediately left the man. The state of decay was turned around instantly. Fingers and toes grew back, ulcers dried up, eyebrows returned, and discolored patches were smoothed away by the touch of Christ.

A "Great Savior" For "Great Sinners"

The hope we have from the leper's story is that it doesn't matter who you are; you're not beyond the breadth of Christ's love. His love is spread wide! There are no untouchables to Him. While the lepers were forced to live outside the city (Lev. 13:45-46), Jesus also went "outside the camp and bore reproach" (Heb. 13:13). He has related to us by becoming man and suffering at the hands of those whom He created. His touch to the leper reveals that the breadth of His love covers all types of people!

John Newton, the author of "Amazing Grace," was a slave trader earlier in his life. When Christ saved him and changed his life, he later said to a friend, "My memory is nearly gone; but I remember two things: that I am a great sinner, and that Christ is a great Savior."[3] Newton realized that the widespread hideous sin in his life was met, touched, and "the record of debt that stood against him" was "nailed to the cross" (Colossians 2:14).

Covered

The condition of the leper was comprehensive in its covering. It was more than just the outer appearance of the man; it was a covering that had deep roots that ran deep through his blood and nerves.

Like leprosy, sin covers the whole person. However, as vast as the covering of sin is, there is a broader covering of God's love. Indeed, where "sin abounds, grace abounds all the more" (Romans 5:20).

Psalm 32 gives a beautiful picture of the love that covers sin:

> Blessed is the one whose transgression is forgiven, whose sin is covered. Blessed is the man against whom the Lord counts no iniquity, and in whose spirit there is no deceit (vv. 1-2).

The end of the Psalm says, "Be glad in the Lord, and rejoice, O righteous, and shout for joy, all you upright in heart!" (Psalm 32:11). We know that no one is naturally "upright in heart." Romans 3 teaches that, "None is righteous, no, not one…for all have sinned and fall short of the glory of God" (v. 10, 23). So how could the Psalmist say, "Be glad in the Lord, and rejoice, O righteous, and shout for joy, all you upright in heart!" (Psalm 32:11)? The reason the Psalmist can say this is because the "righteous" and "upright in heart" people are "those whose transgression is forgiven, whose sins are covered" (Psalm 32:1-2).[4]

The vast nature of our sin is covered by the vast nature of His love. The widespread sickness is remedied by the widespread love of Christ!

The Star Of The Story

My son Owen loves trains. He wants to play with them all the time. I know more about trains now than I've ever known, and I've learned it from spending time with my two-year old-son. The other day, I went into his room while he was playing with these locomotives on his train table. I looked at the ten-car Thomas train that he had built and quickly noticed that there were some trains missing. He has three "Percy" trains, and none were accounted for in this impressive train. I looked at Owen, and said, "Where's Percy?"

Owen walked around the table and opened up a little compartment and said, "Percy's in here." I realized that in Owen's imaginative playtime, Percy was not the star of his story that day…Thomas was.

In the story of our lives, there's already a Star to the story and He's the Star everyday. Christ was, is, and forever will be the Star. When we hear the Gospel and the incredible nature of Christ's love for us, we could be guilty of thinking that we're the center of attention. This is not the case. Ultimately, His love for us is for His own glory: "I, I am He who blots out your transgressions for My own sake, and I will not remember your sins" (Isaiah 43:25). As Louie Giglio says, "The story already has a Star, and the Star is not you or me."[5]

Conclusion

One thing I wasn't good at as a teacher was using a blackboard, mostly because my handwriting isn't acceptable to people. There was also the added chill-bump producing friction of chalk against the board that my poor little epidermis couldn't handle very often, not to mention the fact that chalk had a way of getting all over my hands and clothes. The thing about chalk is that it isn't seen very well if you use it on white paper. It's best seen against the backdrop of a blackboard.

This is what I hope the leper shows us with the love of Christ. It is against the backdrop of the breadth of our condition that the breadth of His surpassing love is best seen. We aren't loved because we're cute and adorable. We get so caught up in outward appearances, but God sees us from the inside out, which can be pretty ugly. We're loved in spite of our condition. We're loved in our condition! On our worst days and best days He loves us still. He has authority, ability and desire to cleanse us from our sin, like He did the leper. Oh the breadth of His love! It covers the broken! It covers the unwanted! It covers the "bandaged and bruised!"[6] We are the lepers; He is the cure!

Father, we pray that according to the riches of Your glory, that we would have the strength to comprehend that the width of Your love is beyond all measure (Ephesians 3:14-19).

Response:

"Here we are. Here we are. The broken and used,
mistreated, abused. Here we are.
Here You are. Here You are. The beautiful one who came
like a Son. Here You are.
So we lift up our voices, we open our hands to cling to the love
that we can't comprehend.
Oh, lift up your voices and lift up your heads to sing of the love
that has freed us from sin.

Here we are. Here we are. Bandaged and bruised,
awaiting a cure. Here we are.
Here You are. Here You are. Our beautiful King bringing relief.
Here You are with us.
So we lift up our voices and open our hands,
let go of the things that have kept us from Him.

He is the one who has saved us. He is the one who forgave us. He
is the one who has come and is coming again.
He's the remedy.

Oh, I can't comprehend. I can't take it all in. Never understand
such perfect love come for the broken and beat, for the wounded
and weak. Oh, come fall at His feet.
He's the remedy! He's the remedy!
So sing, sing, You are the one who has saved us.
You are the one who forgave us. You are the one who has come
and is coming again to make it alright. Oh, to make it alright.
You're the remedy! Oh, in us You're the remedy

Let us be the remedy. Let us bring the remedy."[7]

Part 3

How Deep

5

How Deep the Pit

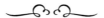

*"I sink in deep mire, where there is no foot-
hold; I have come into deep waters, and
the flood sweeps over me...Deliver me from
sinking in the mire; let me be delivered from
my enemies and from the deep waters. Let
not the flood sweep over me, or the deep
swallow me up, or the pit close its mouth
over me."* –Psalm 69:2, 14-15

*"I am counted among those who go down to
the pit."* –Psalm 88:4

*"He drew me up from the pit of destruction,
out of the miry bog."* –Psalm 40:2

Pitfall Harry

When I was a kid, my family used to have an Atari VCS 2600. I don't think it was the first gaming system, but it was the first one I remember. It preceded the onslaught of gaming systems to come: Nintendo, Sega Genesis, Super Nintendo, Sony Playstation, Sega Saturn, Nintendo 64, Dreamcast, Nintendo Game Cube, Microsoft X-Box, PS2, X-Box 360, PS3 and Nintendo Wii. Despite the obvious advancements in graphics and gameplay in the newer systems, there were some pretty incredible games on the Atari. We had sweet games like, "Skiing" and "Frogger," and another game with helicopters in it, but the best game by far was one called "Pitfall."

The setting of "Pitfall" is deep in the heart of a jungle. The person playing the game controls Pitfall Harry as he tries to maneuver his way through the dangers of the Amazon. He encounters manifold dangers on his journey, which consists of moving from left to right on the screen. When he got to the far right of the screen, he would disappear only to reappear back on the left side with a new treacherous scene placed before him, always endangering his life. He faced crocs, scorpions, rolling logs, things set ablaze, snakes, tar pits, holes, and the one that freaked me out the most: quicksand. The quicksand would appear and retract, but if Pitfall Harry got caught in it, he could not escape. Apparently he hadn't watched "Man vs. Wild," where Bear Grylls shows people how to escape quicksand if God-forbid they ever face it. Harry didn't even put forth an effort to wriggle his way out onto the surface of it and monkey-crawl his way across it; he would just sink and die.

When I read the Psalmist talking about sinking in deep mire (Ps. 69:2, 14-15; 40:2), I sometimes picture the cold, miry quicksand that Pitfall Harry encountered. I played the game enough to know that what was valuable to Harry in those times of sinking beneath the surface was simply a breath of air. Underneath the surface of the quicksand, one breath of air was more valuable to him than all the flatscreens, iPhones and Wiis in the world. We know what it's like to feel like we're sinking. We may not need a breath of fresh air like Harry, but we do need to know that God knows our situations and cares for us.

When God Seems Silent

It's not uncommon for us to feel like we're in a sinking pit when circumstances start acting as parasites attached to us. What's worse than the circumstances building up against us is the polluted idea of trying to measure God's love by what's happening around us. The "pit" happens when nothing in the present circumstances gives us any evidence of His love. All the circumstances really seem to do is clobber us around like a rag doll, and this is when we often begin to feel as if we're sinking into miry clay without the notice of God.

One of my worst nightmares as a kid consisted of me falling from a balcony at the Biltmore house in Asheville, NC. In my dream, my parents, my brothers and I took a trip to tour the Biltmore house. Everything on the trip was fine and dandy until suddenly I lost my balance on a balcony outside. I fell with my back turned toward the ground and my face skyward. It felt like slow motion in my dream. As if falling off a balcony and plummeting to my sure death wasn't bad enough, then add to that the frustration of seeing my two brothers leaning over the balcony laughing at me. What kind of reaction is that? They didn't even try to help me! When I woke up in the morning, I was much more angry over the lack of concern from my brothers than the fall itself.

This is the experience of so many who suffer through hard times. If it isn't bad enough going through the tough circumstances to begin with, then add to that the frustration of feeling ignored by God. We feel like He doesn't care that we're falling into a pit! We agree with David when he says, "How long, O Lord? Will you forget me forever? How long will you hide your face from me?" (Psalm 13:1).

C.S. Lewis describes this feeling when writing about the loss of his wife in "A Grief Observed":

> Where is God?...Go to Him when your need is desperate, when all other help is vain, and what do you find? A door slammed in your face, and a sound of bolting and double bolting on the inside after that, silence. You may as well turn away. The longer you wait, the more emphatic that silence will become...

Why is He…so very absent a help in time of trouble?[1]

Thankfully, the Bible doesn't gloss over this kind of pain as if it doesn't happen. In fact, the Bible is raw and honest in its portrayal of those who are in the lowest of points.

Psalm 77 reveals the raw and honest questions of one who was in a low place:

Will the Lord reject forever? Will He never show His favor again? Has His unfailing love vanished forever? Has His promise failed for all time? Has God forgotten to be merciful? Has He in anger withheld His compassion? (vv. 7-9).

These are the questions that arise during times of personal suffering. Like the writer of this Psalm, our emotions begin to question unseen truth. At times, our emotions can be sweet companions or bitter enemies. Something can happen for instance, like spilled coffee or car trouble that can pull the loose thread on our feelings and begin an unfurling for which we were ill prepared.

It's amazing how much of an effect emotions can have. For instance, imagine one day you come in from work, and as soon as you come in the door, the phone rings. You quickly lay what you're holding onto the couch and run to answer the phone. As you're on the phone, you're not really thinking about what you're doing, and so you lay your keys on a nearby bookshelf, rather than in their normal place. After getting off the phone, you carry on with the rest of your evening at home.

The next morning comes, and you're running a little behind because you had to change clothes because of a stain on your shirt that you noticed. You gather what you need for the day; say your good-byes as you head out the door, and reach to grab your keys...except, your keys aren't there. You turn around and yell, "Hey, has anyone seen my keys?" Your question is met with silence, which adds to the frustration. You glance at the clock only to notice that it refuses to slow down to help you out in your time of need. You search around for your keys, rampaging organized places to see if they've somehow been moved there. You still can't find them, and you yell again this time with a pretty sharp tone, "Who moved my keys!?" While your yell was effective in being heard this time, it wasn't appreciated. "No one moved your keys!" comes a sharp reply back. Within five minutes, you've had to change your shirt because of a stain, you're running late for work, someone obviously moved your keys so now you can't find them, and now your family is upset at you for being frustrated about not being able to leave for work!

Although the day has started off terrible, and your emotions are fiery and frustrated, no circumstance has really changed from the day before. The keys are exactly where you laid them on the bookshelf. The truth of the situation hasn't changed at all. Only your emotions to the situation have changed, but the two days couldn't feel any more different. This is an example of how emotions can be a bitter enemy. Our emotions sometimes look at reality through a lens that is not always accurate.

My pastor recently observed how we often feel the most anxiety when we feel like something is out of our control. He went on to point out that we're not in any more control on the 'good days' than on the 'bad days.' One day we may have anxiety because of car trouble which causes some financial stress, and thus makes us feel a little bit like we're not in as much control as we want to be. However, the day before when the car was running fine, we had no more control over it than the day it wasn't. It's funny how our emotions can sometimes get the best of us. One of my wife's favorite verses is 1 Peter 5:5-7: "Humble yourselves under the mighty hand of God so that at the proper time He may exalt us, casting all our anxieties on Him, because He cares for us." This is the remedy to the anxieties we all face.

A Storm

> When evening came, His disciples went down to the sea, got into a boat, and started across the sea to Capernaum. It was now dark, and Jesus had not yet come to them. The sea became rough because a strong wind was blowing...they had rowed about three or four miles... (John 6:16-19a).

Some of the most beautiful lessons that God has to teach us as believers can only be learned in the hard times. It is in love that Jesus sends His disciples out onto a boat without Him. It might not seem very loving, but Jesus was teaching His disciples, and this particular lesson would only be learned at a time like this. As the Puritan F.W. Faber wrote, "Desertions are not the interruptions of God's love, they are rather the act of God's love."[2]

In the context of this story, there are thousands of people who want to make Jesus king. From the disciples' perspective, they're probably pretty excited about this. Jesus turns earthly kingship down, tells His disciples to get into a boat and cross the sea, and He leaves them, retreating away to a mountain to pray. The disciples begin to cross the Sea of Galilee, which is not a very big sea; it's only about eleven miles long and eight miles wide. It wasn't uncommon for storms to pick up in this sea. Since it's below sea level, winds come down and strike up storms fairly frequently, and although the storms were frequent, they would come quickly and catch people off guard.

The disciples quickly find themselves in a great storm, struggling to make it three or four miles out into the sea. This event takes place later the same evening after Jesus feeds five thousand people. When Jesus finally does come walking on the sea out to His disciples, it's some time between three a.m. and six a.m. This was not a short, enjoyable row into the sea, but rather an eight to ten hour struggle through a fierce storm. The disciples only make it a few miles revealing that they're basically treading water, getting nowhere.

Imagine what this looked like. Picture a little boat getting hammered by a storm, with twelve grown men who are absolutely soaked. I remember one night Jennifer, Owen and I went to a talent show at the school where I taught and while we were inside, a storm came. I knew it was raining hard, so I told Jennifer I would pick them up at the front. By the time I got to the car, which wasn't that far away, it looked like I had taken a quick dip in the neighborhood pool with all my clothes. The disciples must have been soaked to the bone with fingers that looked like raisins. They were in the middle of a dark, hard, difficult storm, and they weren't getting anywhere. They were experiencing dark circumstances. Nothing at the present time was informing them of Christ's love for them.

Imagine what they're thinking. Put yourself in their shoes. John 6:18 says, "The sea became rough because a strong wind was blowing." The storm kicked up and the disciples were in the middle of it for hours, with no sign of Jesus. They can't see him. All they can see are the circumstances that surround them. Jesus could probably see them since He was up on the mountain praying, but they didn't see Him. It's true for many of us that when we're surrounded by dark circumstances we don't see Him. We don't understand why what's taking place is taking place.

Between verse eighteen and nineteen, which says that Jesus came to them, think about what kind of conversations the disciples were having. Earlier that day, they had seen Jesus feed five thousand people. It was a huge, hungry crowd. The disciples watched as

Jesus simply took two little fish and five biscuits and multiplied them to feed the hungry mass. It was truly miraculous. When the people were done eating, the disciples gathered twelve baskets full of leftovers. They probably took the twelve baskets onto the boat with them. I think Jesus was giving them individual object lessons of who He was. Each disciple had a basket full of leftovers to carry as a reminder of how He was able to provide.

Not only that, but Jesus has calmed this particular sea before (Luke 8:22-25). They had been out on a boat with Him on this sea in a storm while Jesus took a nap. The fearful disciples woke Him up saying things like, "Don't you care about us Jesus?" He wakes up and rebukes the wind and waves, and calms the storm. The disciples know what He can do. They've seen Him calm a storm before on this same exact sea, but here, there's no sign of Jesus. They're in the middle of a storm, and they don't know where He is. Imagine what kind of thoughts are going through their heads, and what kinds of complaints are coming out of their mouths during this time: "Where's Jesus?" "Doesn't He care about us?" "He sent us out onto the sea into a storm, and we've been treading water for hours upon hours, what in the world...where is He?"

So often we get into a situation where we find ourselves in a very similar place. Hard times hit and we say, "Where is God? Where is He?" You get a phone call with heart-numbing news, and you feel like you can't stop crying because your soul's been so squeezed by what it's heard. You begin to ask, "Where are you God?" You worry. You doubt. You fear. Disbelief grips your heart. This was the situation in which the disciples had found themselves.

God Moves In Mysterious Ways

There's an old hymn-writer named William Cowper who wrote a song called, "God Moves In A Mysterious Way." William Cowper struggled through a very difficult life. His mother passed away when he was six years old, and his father sent him away to live with other relatives. He struggled with depression throughout his entire life. His pastor, John Newton, the author of "Amazing Grace," came alongside of Cowper and encouraged him. But even after decades of encouragement, Cowper still struggled with dark depression.

One night, he decided he was going to end it all. He couldn't figure out where God was, and he was tired of the struggle. Cowper was a believer, but just didn't know where God was in his pain. He got a cabbie to come to his place and take him to the London Bridge.[3] His plan was to jump off of the bridge and put an end to all his troubles that night. When the cabbie got there and they set off for London Bridge, a thick fog set in. The cabbie couldn't see where to go. He drove around, but he just got lost, and after about an hour, the fog finally lifted, only to reveal that they were in front of William Cowper's house. They hadn't gone anywhere! William Cowper got out and went back into his house. Upon returning to his house that night, he read Psalm 77, and then penned the words to this hymn:

Ye fearful saints fresh courage take! The clouds ye so much dread are big with mercy, and shall break in blessings on your head. Judge not the Lord by feeble sense, but trust Him for His grace; behind a frowning providence, He hides a smiling face.[4]

Jesus said, "In this world we will have trouble" (John 16:33). Peter says, "Don't be surprised at the fiery ordeal that comes upon you" (1 Peter 4:12). Within the storm, trust Him for His grace.

John Bunyan spent twelve years in Bedford prison. He could've gotten out if only he had agreed to stop preaching. He could've been back at home with his family. He had a blind daughter named Mary that he could've been with, but did not because God had called him to preach. While in Bedford prison, he wrote "Pilgrim's Progress," which providentially has been used in the lives of countless people. During this time, he described how prison was having this affect on him of ridding him of love for this world. While we want to avoid hard times, most of us would admit that it's those very same hard times that make us not fall in love with this world.

Owen has a pair of velcro sandals that he loves to wear. I've noticed recently that the velcro is starting to wear down on them, and they'll soon be obsolete, those little tabs just sticking straight up into the air. He walks through mulch, then the mulch gets into the velcro, and then the velcro doesn't stick as well. I think this is the way trials work in our lives. When we go through hard times, our attachment to this world starts to wear down like worn down velcro. The book of Hebrews says, "For here we have no lasting city. We seek the city that is to come" (Hebrews 13:14). Pits, storms and valleys describe the geography of the land where we'll learn the truth of Hebrews 13:14.

We've got to realize that hard times will come. We can't be surprised when they happen. Our lives will be littered full of them. There will be times when we find ourselves in the pit, and there will be times when we find ourselves struggling through a dark storm. Things won't always work out the way we planned or hoped. We'll have disappointments. We'll have struggles. It is in those times that we must have faith and not be blinded by the circumstances.

You're Not Alone

Many believers have experienced hard times. It's easy to sometimes start comparing ourselves with others who seemingly have it all together. We compare their situations to ours, and we get the messed up idea that God must care for them more than He cares for us. What's interesting about this misconception is that we completely make it up. It reminds me of a kid's song called "Fake Believe." It's "fake believe" to assume that the circumstances of life serve as the barometer of God's love for us. Scripture doesn't teach us this. Some modern proponents of a prosperity gospel teach garbage like this, but not Scripture.

Scripture tells us of those who followed God and suffered greatly. It tells us the story of Job who "was blameless and upright, one who feared God and turned away from evil" (Job 1:1), yet suffered the loss of animals, servants, his own children and his personal health. None of the circumstances surrounding him revealed God's love to him, and yet God's love wasn't absent.

The Bible also tells the story of Joseph who was thrown into a literal pit by his brothers, sold into slavery, and eventually put into prison in Egypt for a crime he did not commit. The circumstances during this time did not provide ample evidence of God's love for him, however, "The Lord was with Joseph and showed him steadfast love" (Gen. 39:21), even in the midst of prison.

One of my favorite stories from the book of Acts involves missionaries who were put into "an inner prison" with their feet "fastened in the stocks" (16:24). If God's love is to be measured by circumstances, then Paul and Silas had little to rejoice in. But God's love isn't determined by what happens to us. Paul and Silas knew this and began to "pray and sing hymns to God" (16:25).

We see from Scripture time and time again that His love is steadfast in the good times and in the bad. The author of Hebrews gives a beautiful seamless picture of the faith of individuals who knew God's love for them on miraculous days and on days of intense suffering:

> And what more shall I say? For time would
> fail me to tell of Gideon, Barak, Samson,
> Jephthah, of David and Samuel and the

prophets- who through faith conquered king-doms, enforced justice, obtained promises, stopped the mouths of lions, quenched the power of fire, escaped the edge of the sword, were made strong out of weakness, became mighty in war, put foreign armies to flight. Women received back their dead by resurrection (Hebrews 11:32-35a).

So far, so good. It's easy to feel loved when you're conquering kingdoms and stopping the mouths of lions, and receiving children back from the dead, but the author of Hebrews continues without skipping a beat:

Some were tortured, refusing to accept release, so that they might rise again to a better life. Others suffered mocking and flog-ging, and even chains and imprisonment. They were stoned, they were sawn in two, they were killed with the sword. They went about in skins of sheep and goats, destitute, afflicted, mistreated- of whom the world was not worthy- wandering about in deserts and mountains, and in dens and caves of the earth (Hebrews 11:35b-38).

These men and women, of whom the world was not worthy, suffered through the worst of circum-stances. Yet their hope was not that God would make life easier, but rather in God Himself.

There will be times when the pit feels deep, and the storm feels fierce. Most of us won't be tortured or spend time in a prison for our faith, but we understand feelings of hopelessness and the unknown. Most of us won't find ourselves about to drown out in the open sea like the disciples on a rickety boat, but we might feel like we're drowning in self-pity and helplessness. There are all kinds of personal struggles: losing someone you love, sickness, loss of a job, pain of a divorce, struggles with singleness, financial hardships, betrayal, not getting what you want, feeling like life is flying out of control, car trouble, break-up of a relationship, struggle with sin, etc. In those times be assured that the lovingkindness of God hasn't abandoned you. You may not see Him, but He sees you. No matter how deep the pit gets, "The eternal God is your dwelling place, and underneath are His everlasting arms!" We come now to the hope of His deep love!

6

"How Firm the Foundation"

"Underneath are the everlasting arms."
–Deuteronomy 33:27

"He drew me up from the pit of destruction,
out of the miry bog, and set my feet upon a
rock, making my steps secure. He put a new
song in my mouth, a song of praise to our
God. Many will see and fear, and put their
trust in the Lord." –Psalm 40:2-3

"I am sure that neither death nor life, nor
angels nor rulers, nor things present nor
things to come, nor powers, nor height nor
depth, nor anything else in all creation, will
be able to separate us from the love of God
in Christ Jesus." –Romans 8:38-39

Rescue

There's a theme park close to where we live called Carowinds. When it gets close to Halloween, they do something there they call 'Scarowinds.' I don't know what takes place, I just know there are billboards all over the place that tell me that something scary is happening at Carowinds. I went to the park about twenty years ago, but have never been back. I haven't purposefully avoided the park, but I certainly haven't made many attempts to get there either. Why you may ask? Allow me to explain.

My memory of that place makes me think that it should be called 'Scarowinds' all year long. I remember going to their water park and getting into a wave pool with what felt like about twenty thousand other kids. I somehow elbowed my way out into the deep part of the pool. My feet didn't touch the bottom, but at least I didn't have fellow kids climbing all over me trying to keep their faces above the water. I don't know if all wave pools work this way or not, but this one took breaks (I assume this was to look for the bodies of those who didn't make it). The waves would go for a while, and then somebody would shut them down for about ten minutes or so. I was floating out in the deep end during a wave break thinking, "My arms and legs are tired... where are those waves?" Then the waves started. The waves were big, and I was worn out already, and I'm not that good of a swimmer anyway. As the waves poured over top of me, and filled my screaming mouth full of heavy water that made me sink even more, I realized I was in a place of grave danger. There was no way I was getting through the mob of others struggling toward the shallow end, so I decided to find my way to the edge and grab the side. Upon arriving at my destination, my heart was full of thankfulness for surviving the wave pool. That lasted for about three seconds until a lifeguard yelled for me to get off the edge and back into the pool. "Lifeguard!?" That dude should've done his job and guarded my life. I'm sure he was just a high schooler there to check out the honeys, but I was a struggling kid and needed some help, and he didn't save me.

"I can't go back out there!" I yelled.

"Get...off...of...the...edge!" he said slowly and intensely as if I was a moron and couldn't grasp what he was saying. He looked serious, mean and scary, and so I went back out into the waves and let them have their way with me until the next break. I continued to swallow big gulps of heavy water, which caused me to sink. It was a real blast feeling the feet of others kick my face while under the water. I eventually fought my way back through the shallow end onto the safe haven of the concrete. My feet could touch, and I was able to breathe again!

I haven't been back to (S)carowinds since. Every once and a while, I'll have an urge for a funnel cake, and I'll think about how it might be fun to go again, but then I quit being dumb.

I felt like I was drowning that day, and things were definitely out of my control. The waves were overtaking me, and what I needed was to be rescued.

For centuries, Christians have written about this experience of perceived neglect from God. Saint John of the Cross described the feeling of abandonment from God as "the dark night of the soul." It is the sick feeling of God's withdrawal. Psalm 13:1 says, "How long, O Lord? Will You forget me forever?" In these seasons of darkness and drowning fear, we pray for rescue. I love the way Psalm 40 speaks of rescue:

> He drew me up from the pit of destruction, out of the miry bog, and set my feet upon a rock, making my steps secure. He put a new song in my mouth, a song of praise to our God. Many will see and fear, and put their trust in the Lord (vv. 2-3).

This is the description of someone who needed help getting help. The picture of feet sinking in a miry bog is gloriously contrasted with the firm footing of a rock. The rescue is so incredible that David makes up a "new song" to sing.

This particular psalm describes the reaction of one who is rescued from a pit. But what about those who aren't rescued? How do they experience the love of Christ while remaining in thick darkness?

Christ In The Storm

> The sea became rough because a strong wind was blowing. When they had rowed about three or four miles, they saw Jesus walking on the sea and coming near the boat, and they were frightened. But He said to them, "It is I; do not be afraid" (John 6:18-20).

Jesus comes walking to them in the midst of the storm. He walks out to them on top of the water through lightning, thunder, big waves, rain and darkness. He could've stopped the storm before He got there. He could've calmed it before He began His walk on the water, and yet He comes to them in the middle of the storm.

Those who know me well know that I love to read dead authors. I may start a Facebook group called "The deader the better." One of my favorites is a guy named Helmut Thielicke. I've always wanted to name something after him. My wife's pregnant right now, but she's not too keen on the idea of naming our little boy Helmut. One day, we may get a dog upon which we could bestow this great name. The reason I love Helmut Thielicke is because he was a great writer. He wrote one of the most comforting things I've ever read about the experiences of personal suffering:

> Jesus Christ did not remain at base headquarters in heaven, receiving reports of the world's sufferings from below and shouting a few encouraging words to us from a safe distance. No, He left the headquarters and came down to us...right down to where we live...There is nothing that He did not endure with us. He understands everything.[1]

Christ comes to us in the storm:

> For we do not have a high priest who is unable to sympathize with our weaknesses, but one

who in every respect has been tempted as we are, yet without sin. Let us then with confidence draw near to the throne of grace, that we may receive mercy and find grace to help in time of need (Hebrews 4:15-16).

It is on that road of suffering where we will experience the presence of Christ. We don't want to go there. We don't look forward to journeying down that path. It would be nice to get a brand new car, drink four-dollar Starbucks drinks every day and have it all together nice and neat. We even pray to get off of the difficult road, but most would say that the place where they recognized the presence of Christ the strongest in their lives was in the midst of suffering. It is in these times that we're more sensitive to the reality that He will "never leave us nor forsake us" (Hebrews 13:5).

To those in the storm, the encouragement is to keep looking for Christ above the tops of those giant waves. Look for Him in the middle of the storm. Immediate rescue may not be the answer that is best for you. It may be that God wants to show you His loving presence right where you are. Trust in His love and care for you.

Finally, as He said to His disciples, "Do not be afraid." Don't be fearful. He knows what you're going through. He's gone through it. That's our God, a great King who didn't look like a king that the world wanted: glamorous and attractive; but a King who wore a crown of thorns that brought bruises and blood, showing how He entered into our suffering.

The Loving Care Of The Shepherd

I recently took a trip to the country of Wales with my church. While we were there, we went to a beautiful beach. When I say beautiful, I mean one like I've never seen before. There were stunning cliffs with lush green grass and fluffy sheep grazing till their little chubby hearts were content. Since I don't see a lot of sheep grazing on beautiful beachfront cliffs very often, I wanted to get my picture made with one of them. They didn't seem very interested in having their picture made with me, so they took off running the other direction. While I was watching them run, I remembered that sheep are supposedly some of the dumbest animals alive (although I imagine a jellyfish has got to be right up there on the list). I was nervous that they might run off of the cliff if they got too scared, or fall down and not be able to get back up again. I've always heard about "cast sheep", meaning that sometimes when they fall, they get turned over on their backs and they're unable to roll back over to get up.

Thankfully, none of the sheep fell over or jumped off the cliff. They just ran for a little bit and then kept eating. A former pastor of mine pointed out how sometimes we're like cast sheep and we need the Shepherd to pick us up again. He described how the wool on a sheep will get really nasty with lice and dirt and grime, and how a shepherd has to dig his hands up underneath the sheep through the dirty wool in order to lift it up again. In light of this condition, "The Lord is my Shepherd...He restores my soul"

(Psalm 23), rings more beautifully. His love reaches us in our deepest places. It finds us in our helpless, filthy condition and uplifts us!

What To Do In The Storm

Reflect

Fall is the best season of the year. I know there are those who disagree, but I don't know how someone could argue against the blue skies, perfect temperatures, leaves changing, Thanksgiving, football games, candy corn in my mouth, pumpkin spice coffee flowing freely, etc... It doesn't get better than autumn. One other added treat to the season is deer jerky. I'm not a hunter, but several of my students loved to go hunting. About four years ago, one of my guys named Chase brought me a bag of homemade deer jerky. I was somewhat skeptical, but to appease the lad, I took a tear into it. Since that time, I can barely look at a deer without wanting someone to shoot him and turn him into jerky. They're beautiful creatures and all, but they just taste so delicious.

The reason I look at a deer that way now is because of my past experience with them. In other words, I know what delicious flavors the deer is capable of. My past experience with them gives me a hope of what my future experience will be.

When we encounter the "dark nights of the soul," we need to reflect upon what God has done for us in the past in order to give us hope of what He's capable of in the present. I think this is why the disciples were given the leftover baskets of bread when Jesus fed the five thousand people. They took their baskets and got into a boat and entered into a terrible storm. After Jesus gets into the boat with them, Mark writes that the disciples "did not understand about the loaves, but their hearts were hardened" (Mark 6:52).

What didn't they understand about the loaves? They didn't understand that Christ was able to provide. When the storm kicked up, they responded with great fear. A little look into the back of the boat would've reminded them that Jesus cares and provides for His children. When facing seasons of great difficulty, we must reflect upon what God has done. After writing about his experience in the pit, David writes,

> You have multiplied, O Lord my God, your wondrous deeds and your thoughts toward us; none can compare with You! I will proclaim and tell of them, yet they are more than can be told (Psalm 40:5).

David had experienced great pain, from both his own sin and outward attacks from people like Saul and Absalom. Instead of allowing his feelings and memories to groan, he recalled the wondrous deeds of God, which were too numerous to be told. When we consider all that He's done for us, our perspective is lifted even in the middle of pain.

Several years ago, I was encouraged to make a gratitude list of all the things that I was thankful for, and then to see if I had a legitimate reason to

111

complain about anything. While it's probably pretty self-explanatory, a gratitude list is a catalog of things for which you are thankful. It's extremely difficult to mope around while you're counting your blessings.

A gratitude list could never be exhaustive. God has done too many wonderful things to be counted! In the dark night of the soul, may God give us a spirit of gratitude and faith! God's faithfulness in the past gives us confidence of His future faithfulness.

Respond

Pray! When David was in the "pit of destruction" he cried out to God. In fact, the rescue comes as an answer to his prayer. "He inclined to me and heard my cry. He drew me up from the pit of destruction" (Psalm 40:1-2). For those who struggle with anxiety, desperation, retaliation, loneliness, a sense of abandonment, etc., the encouragement is to cry out to God for help.

The other essential part of responding is to praise God. As Job says, "The Lord gave, and the Lord has taken away; blessed be the name of the Lord" (1:21). David says in Psalm 40:3, "He put a new song in my mouth, a song of praise to our God. Many will see and fear, and put their trust in the Lord." Praising God in the midst of a storm takes the focus off of us and reminds us of the goodness of His providence.

Trust

During times of suffering we often find ourselves far more dependant upon God. It is in the middle of these times that our faith is tested. We know that God is in control, and that He has a plan for what He allows to happen. C.S. Lewis wrote about the necessity of trials in our lives:

> I am progressing along the path of life in my ordinary contented condition, when suddenly a stab of pain threatens serious disease, or a newspaper headline threatens us all with destruction.
>
> At first I am overwhelmed, and all my little happinesses look like broken toys. And perhaps, by God's grace, I succeed, and for a day or two become a creature consciously dependent on God and drawing its strength from the right sources. But the moment the threat is withdrawn, my whole nature leaps back to the toys.
>
> Thus the terrible necessity of tribulation is only too clear. God has had me for but 48 hours and then only by dint of taking everything else away from me. Let Him but sheathe the sword for a minute, and I behave like a puppy when the hated bath is over- I shake myself as dry as I can and race off to reacquire my comfortable dirtiness in the nearest flowerbed.

And that is why tribulation cannot cease until God sees us remade.[2]

Let us trust that God has a plan for us during the difficult seasons. He has us in these places because He loves us. The trials aren't signs of abandonment, they are the signs of a loving Father who is shaping and molding us into the image of His Son (Romans 8:28-29). In these dark seasons, we can rejoice that God has a plan for it. Andrew Murray summarizes:

I am here, (1) By God's appointment, (2) In His keeping, (3) Under His training, (4) For His time.[3]

In the pits and the storms, we must remind ourselves of the hope that He has given to us:

For I am sure that neither tribulation nor distress nor persecution nor famine nor nakedness nor sword nor death nor life nor angels nor rulers nor things present nor things to come nor powers nor height nor depth nor anything else in all creation will be able to separate you from the love of God in Christ Jesus (Romans 8:35, 38-39).

Wait

"I waited patiently for the Lord" (Psalm 40:1). Sometimes the wait is longer than others. Some go through storms for hours, others for decades. While waiting is difficult, it is a God-glorifying action of trust. Waiting shows dependence. The Psalmist must wait on the Lord because he can't move forward without Him. He needs the Lord. Waiting is an acknowledgment of helplessness and an acknowledgement of hopefulness. The circumstances are out of our control, and so we're helpless to change them. However, we wait upon the Lord because He is able to change things.

Helping Others In The Pit

When those around us face times of being in a pit or going through a storm, the best comfort that we can give is not with our mouths, but rather with our presence. I say this only because we tend to be sorry comforters. While in the pit, people need to be loved. They need someone to weep with them (Romans 12:15). Giving reasoned accounts of why God has them in a particularly hard place at present is often as comforting as salt in an open sore. Job's friends tried this approach and failed miserably. A silent, compassionate, tearful presence is much more comforting than oral essays illuminating the reasons as to why someone is experiencing personal suffering.

Conclusion

Suffering is an unavoidable reality in a fallen world. Live long enough, and you will suffer.[4] All of us have experienced some kind of storm or at the very least have had those whom we love experience severe storms. They will come (John 16:33; Acts 14:22; Romans 8:17; Philippians 1:29). It will be during these times that we recognize the exceeding depth of His love. No matter how deep the pit is, no matter how much the bog sinks, there is a solid foundation underneath. So the next time you enter into a sinking pit, remember how firm the foundation is because of His everlasting arms underneath (Deuteronomy 33:27). His love is deep!

Father, we pray that according to the riches of Your glory, that we would have the strength to comprehend that the depth of Your love is beyond all measure (Ephesians 3:14-19).

Response:

"How firm a foundation, ye saints of the Lord,
Is laid for your faith in His excellent Word!
What more can He say than to you He hath said
Who unto the Savior for refuge have fled?

In every condition, — in sickness, in health,
In poverty's vale, or abounding in wealth,
At home and abroad, on the land, on the sea, —
The Lord, the Almighty, Thy strength e'er shall be.

Fear not, I am with thee, oh, be not dismayed,
For I am thy God and will still give thee aid;
I'll strengthen thee, help thee, and cause thee to stand,
Upheld by My righteous, omnipotent hand.

When through the deep waters I call thee to go,
The rivers of sorrow shall not overflow;
For I will be with thee thy troubles to bless
And sanctify to thee thy deepest distress.

When through fiery trials thy pathway shall lie,
My grace, all-sufficient, shall be thy supply.
The flames shall not hurt thee; I only design
Thy dross to consume and thy gold to refine.

E'en down to old age all My people shall prove
My sovereign, eternal, unchangeable love;
And when hoary hairs shall their temples adorn,
Like lambs they shall still in My bosom be borne.

The soul that on Jesus hath leaned for repose
I will not, I will not, desert to his foes;
That soul, though all hell should endeavor to shake,
I'll never, no never, no never, forsake!"[5]

Part 4

Such Great Heights[1]

7

"How Long O Lord?"

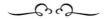

"Why does the way of the wicked prosper?"
–Jeremiah 12:1

"How long, O Lord, must I call for help,
but You do not listen? Or cry out to You,
"Violence!" but You do not save? Why do
You make me look at injustice? Why do You
tolerate wrong? Destruction and violence
are before me; there is strife, and conflict
abounds." –Habakkuk 1:2-3

This will be an uncomfortable chapter to read. It is my hope to paint the background for the height of God's love by looking at the reality of evils in this world. Already, this should raise some eyebrows. The reality of evils within our world are most often used to suggest that God is not loving, rather than providing evidence of His love. The previous section of this book explored personal suffering and the depth of God's love to the individual in the midst of that heartache. This chapter will look at evil on a much larger scale. Evil seems to be like a giant umbrella that covers over the entire world. One needs only to turn the TV to a news channel to realize the far-reaching effects of evil throughout our world. In spite of the fact that moral absolutes are largely rejected in our society, scarcely anyone would deny that there are indeed evils that occur. In other words, the post-modern mindset of suggesting that what's immoral to one person may be perfectly moral to another person falls into a pretty tangled mess when dealing with the obvious evils that take place. David Wells notes:

> How many postmoderns who say there are no moral absolutes would actually think the rape of a small, innocent girl is not morally wrong? That it is not a moral outrage? That it is not always and everywhere wrong? How many would brush off the Nazi concentration camps, or Pol Pot's killing fields in Cambodia, as just misdirected social policy that, unfortunately, didn't work out?[1]

Certainly the world seems very chaotic, which raises some obvious questions about God's involvement within it. I took a class in seminary several years ago called "The Problem of Evil". It was probably the most thought-provoking class I've ever had. In it we read, studied, and debated the arguments surrounding God's involvement in the sufferings of the world. Basically, there are two primary arguments that atheists have against God from evil. However, it's not just atheists that struggle with these questions. Indeed, if we're honest with ourselves, many of us have struggled with these same issues. One is a logical argument, which deals with the tension between the following three statements:

1. God is all-powerful
2. God is all-good
3. Evil exists

Those who argue against God's existence from this logic, reason that these three propositions can't all be true. One of the most well-known statements on the logical problem of evil comes from eighteenth-century philosopher, David Hume,

Is [God] willing to prevent evil, but not able? Then is He impotent? Is He able, but not willing? Then is He malevolent. Is He both able and willing? Whence then is evil?[2]

While the logical argument has been a focus for years and provides a great dialogue in the academy, the other argument is the one with which most people struggle. It is the evidential/experiential argument against God from evil. Those who argue from this perspective simply point at the evils of the world as evidence against God. It's not so much of a logical issue for them as much as it is personal. Tim Keller writes about this idea in his book "Reason for God." He starts a chapter by quoting a girl he had conversed with on the subject of suffering:

"I just don't believe the God of Christianity exists," said Hillary, an undergrad English major. "God allows terrible suffering in the world. So he might be either all-powerful but not good enough to end evil and suffering, or else he might be all-good but not powerful enough to end evil and suffering. Either way the all-good, all-powerful God of the Bible couldn't exist."[3]

Many hold her viewpoint of God: that since there is so much suffering in the world, the Christian understanding of an all-powerful and all-loving God simply must not be true. Admittedly, it wasn't easy to sit and listen to the horrors that were presented in that class as evidence against the attributes of God. I often left feeling somewhat sick to my stomach. We read books and articles chronicling the evils of the world as evidence against the existence of God. It's not easy to hear about genocides, rapes, natural disasters and suffering children.

However, I don't think that a Christian has to tuck his head into the sand and ignore the evils that take place; in fact I think it's not wise to do so in our present era. Perhaps those in the past didn't have to deal with the painful subject of evil in the world as much as we do. Not because there was a lack of evils, but rather because they weren't presented with it through means of television, computers, radios and newspapers. It's very difficult, in our world, to avoid the issue that numerous and intense evils take place on a regular basis. One only has to turn on the news to find something horrible. Even within the past couple of days, I've seen the great loss people have experienced because of Hurricane Ike. I've also seen coverage of a train wreck in California that resulted in the death of at least twenty-five people. These events took place just within the United States; surely the troubles are multiplied numerous times over throughout the world. It's not like you have to look far to find examples of evil; just watch your local news to hear about car wrecks, break-ins and other tragedies. Examples of suffering are painfully present. Michael Peterson writes:

> Something is dreadfully wrong with our world. An earthquake kills hundreds in Peru. A pancreatic cancer patient suffers prolonged, excruciating pain and dies. A pit bull attacks a two-year-old child, angrily ripping his flesh and killing him. Countless multitudes suffer the ravages of war in Somalia. A crazed cult leader pushes eighty-five people to their deaths in Waco, Texas. Millions starve and die in North Korea as famine ravages the land. Horrible things of all kinds happen in our world- and that has been the story since the dawn of civilization. Today's news media thrive on things that are wrong in the world, on bad things that happen to people every

day. Television parades vivid images of war, murder devastation, and suffering before our eyes. Newspapers report rape, abuse, mayhem, and disaster.[4]

In what follows, I simply want to list some of the evils that are present within our world, and the questions that arise from them. I'll seek to address a proper response to them in the chapter to follow. For the sake of clarity, we'll examine three categories of evils: natural, moral and physical. I make the distinction only to acknowledge that some evils are brought about by people, while others are beyond the ability of man.

Natural Evils

Indeed, there is "something dreadfully wrong with our world." A natural evil is defined as an event that "does not involve human willing and acting, but is merely an aspect of nature that seems to work against human welfare."[5] Events like hurricanes, floods, droughts, earthquakes and mudslides can't be blamed on the ill motives of people.

On December 26th, 2004, an earthquake in the Indian Ocean caused a tsunami to hit the coasts of Indonesia, Thailand, Sri Lanka, India, and even parts of Africa. Almost a quarter of a million people were killed in the tragedy, and millions were left homeless. The numbers are difficult to take in, but the reality of individuals and families that make up those numbers are even more affecting. Sometimes the portrayal of numbers that come through reports on TV have a way of making these types of sufferings very impersonal, but the truth is that these events affect real people, like you and me, who have suffered the loss of loved ones. Imagine your situation if the tsunami had hit where you live right now.

In 2005, Hurricane Katrina hit the Gulf Coast of the United States devastating thousands of families. The levees didn't hold in New Orleans, which put most of the city under water. A few weeks ago Hurricane Ike hit the Gulf Coast leaving at least fifty people dead, devastating damage and millions without power.

A mudslide in Venezuela kills over fifteen thousand people. A tornado destroys a family's first home in Oklahoma. A drought leaves millions in China with water shortages. A fire caused by lightning leaves a family with nothing. A cyclone hits Myanmar, killing 146,000 people. A daughter is killed in an accident because of rainy conditions. Nature has certainly caused much mayhem for humanity. So much so, that it has caused some to abandon their hope in God:

> God, if there is a God, should be ashamed of Himself. The sheer enormity of the Asian tsunami disaster, the death, destruction, and havoc it has wreaked, the scale of misery it has caused, must surely test the faith of even the firmest believer…I hope I am right that there is no God. For if there were, then He'd have to shoulder the blame. In my book, He

would be as guilty as sin and I'd want nothing
to do with Him."[6]

Moral Evils

People like Stalin, Hitler and Mao Tse-Tung
have committed crimes against humanity that have
resulted in the deaths of millions of people. The
horrors that have recently taken place in Africa are
difficult to even process:

- Over 500,000 people killed in Angola in the
  past 20 years.
- 45,000 people die each month in the
  Democratic Republic of Congo, with children
  accounting for about half of those deaths.
- The two-year border war between Eritrea and
  Ethiopia caused the death of about 100,000
  people.
- The genocide that took place in Rwanda in
  the conflict between the Tutsis and Hutus.
- The crisis in Darfur has resulted in the death
  of hundreds of thousands of people, and over
  a million Sudanese displaced in the past 5
  years.[7]

On April 16, 2007, Seung-Hui Cho went on a
shooting rampage on the campus of Virginia Tech.
It ended with Cho taking his own life after killing
thirty-two other students. It was the deadliest school
shooting in U.S. history. About two hours after
killing two students in a dorm, he cleaned himself

up, and walked into Norris Hall with a backpack full of chains, locks, guns and ammunition. He locked the doors and began to open fire into classrooms. The questions of "Why?" began to pour out onto the headlines of newspapers and magazines throughout the world.

Several years ago, I remember reading about a five-year old girl named Sue who was followed into a bathroom, raped, beaten and murdered by strangulation. I recently heard about a couple that hung their baby up in the air and put cigarettes out on her body. I read another story about a twelve-year old boy whose parents kept him in his room with no furniture and only a bucket to relieve himself. He spent his days and nights on a linoleum floor alone. His parents neglected him except for the times when they came and whipped him with extension cords and other torturous things. It's too much to take in. It really does make you want to throw up when you read things like this. I feel a little bit like Ivan from Dostoevsky's novel, "The Brothers Karamazov":

> Listen, I took the case of children only to make my case clearer. Of the other tears of humanity with which the earth is soaked from its crust to its center, I will say nothing. I have narrowed my subject on purpose.[8]

The moral evils that take place are truly too numerous to consider, so much so, that no sane person would deny their existence. Every day is full of ample evidence of the depravity of man. Every day is full of enough pain to smudge the ink of the local newspaper with our tears.

Physical Evils

On top of the natural and moral evils, there are still others to consider such as AIDs, hunger, lack of clean water, cancer, disease, suffering in old age, etc. Every day millions of people face complicated situations due to the physical sufferings in our world.

A few days ago we went to Tennessee to visit our families. We used to drive out to a little town called Kingsport to visit my grandfather, but now he lives in a nursing home close to where my parents live. It's hard to see him struggle to communicate. His cheeks are sunken and his hands are lean. I understand the frustration of seeing a loved one diminished to a shell of who they once were. The common reaction is "Why?" Why does God allow a person like my grandfather to physically suffer?

The reality of evil within our world is indeed difficult to deny. The differences of opinion come largely from the responses to these evils.

Questions

There are several questions that arise when great evils occur. When something like a natural disaster occurs, resulting in the loss of hundreds of lives, we see these kinds of questions splattered across the fronts of newspapers. The first question is, "Where is God in all of this?" When things are good, God doesn't get much press, but when something bad happens, everyone wants to know where He is. The second question is, "Is He good?" With all the problems in the world like hunger, thirst, cancer, AIDS, and genocide, can God be trusted as good? The last question is, "Is He really in control?" It's the idea that "maybe God really is good, but He just can't do anything about it." I hope to thoughtfully respond to these questions in the next chapter, but for now I simply want to acknowledge the reality of these questions, often sincerely asked.

Where is God?

I sat in a class one day as a professor came in and silently wrote on the chalkboard: Godisnowhere. He turned around and asked for someone to raise his hand and tell the class what he saw. Someone spoke up and said, "God is nowhere." The professor then asked if anybody else saw something different. A hand went up and a student replied, "I thought it said, 'God is now here.'" It's interesting how people can look at the same situation and come away with such different explanations. For many people, the world's tragedies produce these two responses. Some feel that God is nowhere, while others experience His presence and can say, "God is now here."

Paul Williams writes about a conversation he had with a New York firefighter recalling the events of a devastating fire.

The firefighter struggled with why God would allow such an evil to occur:

Three years ago, there was a fire six stories up- one bedroom apartment, fifteen people living in it- and I find a little girl. Hurt pretty bad, holding a kitten. So I bring her down, six stories, She's crying at me the whole time, saying, "Please Mr. Fireman, please save my kitten, please don't let anything happen to my kitten, Mr. Fireman." Anyway, long story short. Cat lived. She didn't...My cousin the priest says it's because it's all part of God's plan, like God's got a plan. You know what? If there is a God, he's got a whole lot of explaining to do.[9]

The question that lies at the heart of this is "Where is God?" "If He exists, where in the world is He?" In my observation, this is the most common argument against the existence of God. It's seems for my generation, it's no longer primarily a scientific debate between evolution and creation, as much as people look at the horrible things within our world as evidence against His existence. It seems for many that the weight of cruelty within the world feeds the perspective of God is nowhere instead of God is now here.

Is God good?

A second question that comes up when evils occur is, "Is it really loving to permit so much evil?" Does God really care about those who are hungry, or those who suffer from wars? It's not a question of His existence as much as it is a question of His goodness. If God exists and is all-powerful, then why does He not stop the suffering?

Some pain makes obvious sense. In fact, pain is a sign of vitality. If a doctor must perform surgery to save a life, then the pain of surgery is surely understandable. Many evils can be quickly explained as a necessary and justified element of living.

It is with those evils that seem devoid of purpose with which people struggle. Why would God allow an infant to be abused? What good could really come from that? Even if there was a good that could come from that sort of horror, how come an all-powerful God can't figure out another way to bring about that good?

If suffering has a reasonable and seeable purpose, then we'll be ok with it. Albeit, it still won't be easy to live through, but at least we can understand. What's difficult is purposeless evil, and why a good God doesn't stop it from happening. I read an article by a guy named William Rowe who used an example of a fawn trapped in a forest fire to raise this same question. In his example, lightning strikes a tree and a fire breaks out in the forest. The fawn is trapped and severely burned, and then several days later the fawn dies. Rowe simply asks, why would God allow something like that to happen? It has no purpose. No one was there to see the deer, so there were no lessons to be learned. All that happened was an innocent deer suffered through intense pain. Wouldn't it be more merciful for a good God to either let the deer escape or at least kill it quickly? Why would a good God allow this purposeless evil to happen?

Is God really in control?

A third question that is raised is, "Is God really in control?" If God exists and He cares for us, then why doesn't He step in and stop the suffering more often? The speculation is that since there is so much chaos in the world, maybe He's not really in control of all that happens.

Even some Christian authors weigh in with this view:

> God simply can't override free wills when-ever they might conflict with His will. Because God decided to create this kind of world, He can't ensure that His will is carried out in every situation. He must tolerate and wisely work around the irrevocable freedom of human and spirit agents.[10]

Is it true that our God must "work around" what man does? Is this the kind of control that He possesses?

Conclusion

In this chapter, I've sought to honestly look at the "great heights" of evil within our world and raise the accompanying difficult questions that follow. Have you ever felt this way, or asked these questions? If not, there are people all around you that probably have. Look around: the waitress at your favorite restaurant; the high school girl in the bookstore; the alternative kid at the movies; your neighbor five houses down the street; or someone in your own family. Surely we all know people who wrestle with these issues.

In the next chapter, I hope to demonstrate through Scripture how God is over all things, and how He is fixing our world. It won't always be the way it is now. This is the metanarrative (the big story that all the little stories make up) of Scripture! God made a good world, and we messed it up with sin. But we look to Christ, the One who delivers us, rescues us and makes all things new!

8

How High His Love

*"Who has spoken and it came to pass,
unless the Lord has commanded it? Is it not
from the mouth of the Most High that good
and bad come?" –Lamentations 3:37-38*

*"Who is like the Lord our God, who is
seated on high." -Psalm 113:5*

*"And we know that for those who love God
all things work together for good, for those
who are called according to His purpose.
For those whom He foreknew He also
predestined to be conformed to the image of
His Son…" –Romans 8:28-29*

Dictionary: Overtop (ō'vər-tŏp')

1. *To extend or rise over or beyond the top of; tower above.*
2. *To take precedence over; override.*
3. *To be greater or better than; surpass.*[1]

In the last chapter, I pictured evil as a giant umbrella that seemingly covers the entire world. Now imagine another umbrella much, much larger overtop of it. You are standing underneath both of them, but can only see the one that is closest to you. Thus, from your perspective the most visible covering is the smaller umbrella. When speaking about the height of God's sovereign love, perhaps this will serve as a helpful image. Overtop of every evil that takes place on this planet is God's sovereign love.

It is not my primary goal within this chapter to seek to demonstrate why God allows evils to occur. Partly, because I'm sure I would fail at trying to do so, but also because I'm not sure that this is what's best for us. It seems that Scripture does less explaining in this realm than it does to the truth that God is over all, and how we should respond to that truth. God has a sovereign plan that is overtop every evil that takes place. With that in mind, I'll follow the weight of Scripture and seek to demonstrate God's sovereign love over all things, and how we should respond to the evils that surround us. In short, I hope to encourage our faith that God has a plan for the seeming chaos of evil.

Christ Over The Storm

"They were glad to take Him into the boat, and immediately the boat was at the land to which they were going" (John 6:21).

Revisiting the story of Jesus coming to His disciples during the storm in John 6, I imagine the disciples were glad to take Him into the boat! When I taught Bible at the Christian school, I taught through the book of John verse by verse every year with my freshman guys' class. The sophomores studied through the book of Acts, and the juniors studied Paul's letter to the Romans. When I left the school, my students went above and beyond in their expressions of love towards me. I couldn't have asked for anything more. My freshman class came up with a great gift idea for me. Each student wrote down his name and beside of it, his favorite verse from the book of John. They presented me with the list on the last day of class and each person stood and explained why they picked the verses they did, and why it meant so much to them. It was very meaningful to me. One of my students wrote John 6:21 as his favorite verse. I had never heard anyone say that verse was his favorite. He stood up and said something along the lines of, "I love the fact that as soon as He got into the boat, immediately the boat got to the other side. That's a miracle I'd never heard before, and it just reminds me of how powerful God is."

He's in control. Omnipotence has no boundaries, and it has no need to hurry. He's in control of all things. At school I used to be in charge of coordinating the praise band. I'm not that musical, so I would just sit in the back and give some instruction on what songs would go well with the message, but other than that, I let them work together to plan the music. Through that experience, I learned how to use the soundboard a little bit. Here's how it went every Wednesday afternoon for praise band practice: "Hey Mr. McMurray, will you turn up the guitar?"

"Sure no problem."

"Hey, will you turn up the vocals too?"

"O.K."

"Is there anyway to turn up the drums?" By the end of practice, everything was pushed all the way up on the soundboard. They just wanted it loud, and as loud as possible.

When I see these two questions, "Is God good?" and "Is He in control?" we sometimes get into a movement of thinking that either God is good, but He's not really in control, or God's powerful, but He doesn't care about me. What I hope for is that the beliefs that God is good and God is in control will both be pushed up to the highest volume possible so that our faith is even stronger. He is good; He does care; and He's absolutely powerful and in control.

Rabbi Kushner, who wrote a very famous book called, "When Bad Things Happen To Good People," said this: "Sometimes it is even too difficult for God to keep cruelty and chaos from claiming innocent victims."[2] However, that's not what Scripture says. This is an unbiblical view. Scripture talks about His sovereignty over all things. In Job 38:8-11, God speaks to Job:

> Who shut in the sea with doors when it burst out from the womb, when I made clouds its garment and thick darkness its swaddling band, and prescribed limits for it and set bars and doors, and said, 'Thus far shall you come, and no farther, and here shall your proud waves be stayed?'

He's the One who tells the waves where to stop. If He lets His hand off of it, they can come further. If He puts His hand down, they stay where He wants them to be. He's in charge of the ocean, and He's in charge of the weather. As Paul writes to Timothy, "God...is the blessed controller of all things" (1 Timothy 6:15). He's in control of those who hunger, those who thirst, and those who are in pain. He's in control of you when you drop your coffee in your lap on your way to work in the morning. He's in control of traffic jams. He's over every drop of rain, every hurricane, every blade of grass, every financial woe, every illness, and every single person. Our God is sovereign:

> Man plans his course, but the Lord determines His steps (Proverbs 16:9).

> The king's heart is in the hand of the Lord; He directs it like a watercourse wherever He pleases (Proverbs 21:1).

He works all things according to the counsel
of His will (Ephesians 1:11).

I always tried to get the students I taught to read
some of the old Puritan writers like John Flavel. They
knew I liked to read the "dead guys" and you can tell
by his language that ole "Flavel Flave" is not of this
era. Concerning God's providence, Flavel wrote:

The affairs of the saints in the world are
certainly conducted by the wisdom and care
of special providence.[3]

He goes on to say:

Oh how ravishing and delectable a sight will
it be to behold at one view the whole design
of Providence, and the proper place and use
of every single act, which we could not understand in this world.[4]

People don't talk this way anymore, but it is so
good! God is sovereign. He's in control of the storm
in which we find ourselves, and He's in control of the
much larger storms that don't personally affect us.
In the parallel passage found in Matthew's Gospel,
after Jesus gets into the boat it says, "Those in the
boat worshipped Him saying, 'Truly You are the Son
of God'" (Matthew 14:33). God is over every storm.
He's the One who says when it begins and when it
ends. His timing is perfect. There are no boundaries
for omnipotence, and there is no frantic rush. He is

high above every event that unfolds, and our best response to this is to worship Him. "Is it not from the mouth of the Most High that good and bad come?" (Lamentations 3:38). As a response to this, "Let us lift up our hearts and hands to God in heaven" (Lamentations 3:41).

However, this is not a common response among those who see injustices and evils as a statement against the nature of God. When something horrible happens, blame is quickly passed to God: "Where is God?" or "Why in the world does He not stop all the suffering?" Some even accuse God of injustice. However, as Dorothy Sayers adequately sets forth, justice is not what we really want:

Why doesn't God smite this dictator dead?" is a question a little remote from us. Why, madam, did he not strike you dumb and imbecile before you uttered that baseless and unkind slander the day before yesterday? Or me, before I behaved with such a cruel lack of consideration to that well-meaning friend? And why sir, did he not cause your hand to rot off at the wrist before you signed your name to that dirty bit of financial trickery? You did not quite mean that? But why not? Your misdeeds and mine are none the less repellent because our opportunities for doing damage are less spectacular than those of some other people. Do you suggest that your doings and mine are too trivial for God to bother about? That cuts both ways; for in that case, it would make precious little difference to his creation if he wiped us both out tomorrow.[5]

We need grace. When one wishes that God would destroy evil, he fails to realize that he's a part of that evil. The truth is that God does have a wonderful plan in carrying out justice (see next chapter).

What Does The Bible Say?

God Is Over Nature

He unleashes His lightning beneath the whole heaven and sends it to the ends of the earth... He says to the snow, "Fall on the earth," and to the rain shower, "Be a mighty downpour"... The breath of God produces ice, and the broad waters become frozen. He loads the clouds with moisture; He scatters His lightning through them. At His direction they swirl around over the face of the whole earth to do whatever He commands them. He brings the clouds to punish men, or to water His earth and show His love (Job 37:3, 6, 10-13).

He covers the sky with clouds; He supplies the earth with rain and makes grass grow on the hills...He spreads the snow like wool and scatters the frost like ashes. He hurls down His hail like pebbles. Who can withstand His icy blast? He sends His word and melts them;

He stirs up His breezes, and the waters flow (Psalm 147:8, 16-18).

Do the skies themselves send down showers? No it is You, O Lord our God. Therefore our hope is in You, for You are the One who does all this (Jeremiah 14:22).

He causes His sun to rise on the evil and the good, and sends rain on the righteous and the unrighteous (Matthew 5:45).

God Is Over People

The king's heart is in the hand of the Lord; He directs it like a watercourse wherever He pleases (Proverbs 21:1).

The Lord moved the heart of Cyrus king of Persia to make a proclamation throughout his realm and to put it in writing (Ezra 1:1).

You intended to harm me, but God intended it for good to accomplish what is now being done, the saving of many lives (Genesis 50:20).

God Is Over Physical Suffering

Who gave man his mouth? Who makes him deaf or mute? Who gives him sight or makes him blind? Is it not I, the Lord? (Exodus 4:11).

"Rabbi, who sinned, this man or his parents, that he was born blind?" Jesus replied, "Neither this man nor his parents sinned but this happened so that the work of God might be displayed in his life" (John 9:2-3).

[God] knit me together in my mother's womb (Psalm 139:13).

The Lord has kept me from having children (Genesis 16:2).

Coming Home From South Africa With A Tick

The secret things belong to the Lord our God, but the things revealed belong to us and to our children forever, that we may follow all the words of this law (Deuteronomy 29:29).

There's a popular assumption that if God allows an evil to occur, we should be able to find an accompanying good that would give reason for it. While I believe that there is good purpose for everything that takes place, I don't think it is reasonable for us to assume that we'll be able to see all those purposes.

Several years ago, I took a trip to South Africa. The team I traveled with went out into Zulu land and camped out in the middle of the bush. While we were there, several people that were on our team got ticks.

The ticks there aren't like the ticks that we have in North Carolina. If a tick gets on you in the States, you'll most likely be able to spot it. The ticks in South Africa were microscopic, and we couldn't really see them until after they had already done their damage. Fortunately for me, I made it through the whole week without any ticks...or so I thought. A couple of days after my return, I noticed a sore on my leg. It started to turn into a little crater. I knew what had happened because I saw several people experience the same thing while we were there...it was a tick.

I thought I made it through the entire trip without any ticks because I didn't see any on me. It reminded me of an article by a guy named John Stephen Wykstra that I once read. In it, he says:

Looking around my garage and seeing no dog entitles me to conclude that none is present, but seeing no flea does not; and this is because fleas, unlike dogs, have low seeability: even if they were present, we cannot reasonably expect to see them in this way. But should we expect God-purposed goods to have the needed seeability?...Imagine a doctor, squinting at a used hypodermic needle and seeing no germs, inferring first that the needle does not appear to have any germs on it, and from this, that it does not have any germs on it. We should, I believe, resist the doctor's inference at the first step: the claim that the needle appears germless is a very big claim quite unwarranted by the doctor's seeing no germs.[6]

Wykstra is arguing against the idea that the good that God might bring out of a bad situation must be seeable. Why would we assume that? Scripture doesn't tell us that we'll be able to see the outworking of God's providence for us. While we're not always able to see how God is working in and through events that occur, we are promised that His loving providence is over all things. Jerry Bridges defines God's providence as, "His constant care for and His absolute rule over all His creation for His own glory and the good of His people."[7] We may or may not see the way this works out in our lives. Of providence, Charles Spurgeon writes:

Providence is wonderfully intricate. Ah! You want always to see through Providence, do you not? You never will, I assure you. You have not eyes good enough. You want to see what good that affliction was to you; you must believe it. You want to see how it can bring good to the soul; you may be enabled in a little time; but you can not see it now; you must believe it. Honor God by trusting Him.[8]

God is sovereign in His love. He knows how to bring about that which is for His glory and for our good. The problem from our perspective is that we don't always know what is ultimately working for

His glory, or working for our good, or even what is best for us. The 'good' that God is working in and for us is that we would be conformed to the image of His Son (Romans 8:29). This may or may not be through adverse circumstances, but the circumstances aren't the most important factor. It is in love that He seeks that which is best for us, and it is in wisdom that He brings it about.

When Jennifer and I used to change Owen's diaper as a baby, he wouldn't always enjoy the process. I suppose in his mind it was frustrating, and to him, it didn't altogether seem to be very loving. He would cry and kick those little legs back and forth, indicating to us that it was not enjoyable. However, in love we sought that which was best for him, and in wisdom we carried it out. Wykstra observed this about our understanding God's purposes for pain:

> [Our understanding is] about as likely as that a one-month-old should discern most of his parents' purposes for those pains they allow him to suffer- which is to say, it is not likely at all.[9]

Throughout Scripture we are taught to trust God. For Christians, this is an essential part of our sanctification: that we would grow in our trust of God. The thing about trust is that it is developed in places where we don't see all that is taking place. If we see everything clearly, then we're walking by sight and not by faith. There's a David Wilcox song that says, "If God gave me a vision, would I ever have reason to use my faith?"[10] In this sense, seeing is not what is best for us. As my pastor says, there is a difference between what is good to me and what is good for me. A Krispy Kreme chocolate-covered cream-filled doughnut is good to me, but it is not good for me.

A couple of months ago, I went to Wales where we held a "Soccer School" for the children in the Cardiff Bay area. We mostly played football with them, but one day we decided to set up an "Olympics" for them. We had about a dozen different games in which they could participate. A whistle would blow and groups would rotate from game to game. I was in charge of leading a game called "cross the river." There was no real river to cross, so I laid out cones in the grass to represent the banks of the river on both sides, so they knew when they had crossed it. In the middle were obstacles that represented danger. If they touched something in the middle of the river, they had to start over. If not for the following bit of information about this game, it would be overly simple. The difficult part of crossing the river was the fact that the kids were blindfolded. Since they couldn't see where they were going, they had to listen, trust and obey the voices of the people within their group.

We had kids ranging from five years old to about twelve years old. When the five-year old group came to my station, I was worried that they wouldn't do as well as the older ones. What I found was the exact opposite. The older kids took off with a bit too much pride, refusing to listen to the instruction of their group, and not really trusting what they heard. Rarely did they make it across the river. On the other hand, almost every single one of the five-year old kids made it across the river.

2 Corinthians 5:7 says, "For we walk by faith, not by sight." The best place for our faith to grow is in the place of not being able to see it all. If we were to see everything clearly, then our faith would be weaker for it.

John The Baptist

Earlier the same day that Jesus calmed the storm with His disciples, He had heard some disturbing news. The one person who had perhaps understood Him the most was killed. Herod had beheaded John the Baptist. We know John was an amazing person because Jesus spoke of Him in this manner: "Among those born of women there has arisen no one greater than John the Baptist" (Matthew 11:11). When Jesus heard the news of the death of His cousin, He "withdrew in a boat to a desolate place by Himself" (Matthew 14:13a). He wasn't allowed to mourn very long however, because "when the crowds heard it, they followed Him on foot from the towns" (Matthew 14:13b). When the crowds met Him on the shore, He had compassion for them, healed the sick, fed five thousand people, and later that night He calmed a storm (and you thought you had a busy day today). In the middle of all the activity, He was mourning the loss of John the Baptist.

What's interesting about the context of what Jesus said about John's greatness is how easy it is to relate to John. Not to his greatness, but rather to his vulnerability. Here's the context:

> Now when John heard in prison about the deeds of the Christ, he sent word by his disciples and said to Him, "Are You the One who is to come, or shall we look for another?" (Matthew 11:2-3).

John had questions. He had doubts. He sat in a prison and wondered about Jesus being the Christ. This should be encouraging to us that even John had his vulnerable moments. I'm not trying to suggest that his greatness was linked with his doubt, but I do think it's noteworthy that his greatness wasn't blemished by his sincere questions. John was suffering because of evil and he wanted to know whether Jesus was the Christ or not. This type of questioning still takes place today. Out of the context of suffering come questions related to God's involvement in the world. Here's how Jesus responded to his questions:

> And Jesus answered them, "Go and tell John what you hear and see: the blind receive their sight and the lame walk, lepers are cleansed and the deaf hear, and the dead are raised up, and the poor have good news preached to them. And blessed is the one who is not offended by Me" (Matthew 11:4-6).

Jesus sent word back to John to have faith. He told John's disciples to bear witness to what they had heard and seen. In the midst of suffering, a great Healing had come! In the midst of darkness, a great Light had come! Note how Jesus responded by using examples of how He came to transform evil into good:

- The blind............................receive their sight
- The lame ....walk
- The lepers ....cleansed
- The deaf...hear
- The dead ....raised up
- The poor... have good news preached to them

Look to Christ, the One who delivers, rescues and makes all things new! This is the same message Jesus preached in His first recorded sermon:

The Spirit of the Lord is upon Me, because He has anointed Me to proclaim good news to the poor. He has sent Me to proclaim liberty to the captives and recovering of sight to the blind, to set at liberty those who are oppressed, to proclaim the year of the Lord's favor (Luke 4:18-19).

His love is higher than any evil that takes place. For the poor, He brings good news. For the captives, He proclaims liberty. For the blind, they receive sight. For the oppressed, liberty! In a world filled with evils, Christ brings salvation.

Jesus' Response To Evil

How would Jesus respond to a question related to the problem of evil? How would He respond to the questions asked on Wednesday morning, September 12th, 2001, the day after the towers of the World Trade Center collapsed?

In Luke 13, Jesus responded to a similar situation. The numbers are different, but the tower of Siloam fell and killed eighteen people, and Jesus responded to the questions of why.

"Those eighteen on whom the tower in Siloam fell and killed them: do you think that they were worse offenders than all the others who lived in Jerusalem? No, I tell you; but unless you repent, you will all likewise perish" (Luke 13:4-5).

His response was to be ready. In other words, since we live in a fallen world, our response to evil is to be ready for it when it happens.

Regarding this truth the Bible says:

"You do not know what tomorrow will bring. What is your life? For you are a mist that appears for a little time and then vanishes" (James 4:14).

"All flesh is like grass and all its glory like the flower of grass. The grass withers and the flower falls, but the word of the Lord remains forever" (1 Peter 1:24-25).

"I tell you, my friends, do not fear those who kill the body, and after that have nothing more that they can do. But I will warn you whom to fear: fear Him who, after He has killed, has authority to cast into hell. Yes, I tell you, fear Him! Are not five sparrows sold for two pennies? And not one of them is forgotten before God. Why, even the hairs of your head are all numbered. Fear not; you are of more value than many sparrows" (Luke 12:4-7).

Jesus responded to evil by telling His listeners to be ready. He didn't answer all of the "why" questions. He didn't tell them that they were being judged for sins they had committed. The tower fell on eighteen people and killed them, therefore be ready.

Conclusion

Whether we see how God has sovereignly worked things for His glory and for our good is not our major concern. Either way, we're called to trust Him. We trust Him by believing His promises. When Jennifer and I were dating, she lived in Asheville and I lived in Raleigh. I often made the four-hour journey at night in the dark. As I traveled, the headlights would light up my path, so that I would see just enough of the road to confidently move forward. I couldn't see the whole journey, only short segments at a time were revealed to me. At the end of the trip, I found that every part of the journey was lit up so that I could reach my destination. I suppose this is a little bit like the way it works with faith. God doesn't show us everything. He doesn't reveal the whole journey to us. He just tells us to keep moving forward in faith.

We know His love is deep and long and wide. It's also higher than the highest heavens. Do we truly believe this in our lives, whether good or bad happens? Or do we measure His love by what we see? He is over all things, and there is nothing that takes place that falls out of the bounds of His sovereign love. He is, as 1 Timothy 6:15 says, "The blessed controller of all things."

The evils in this world, whether from nature, people, or physical suffering, reach high to the heavens. They compose a very large umbrella that seemingly covers everything. However, we must believe that God's love is higher than the highest heavens, and it composes a much larger umbrella that encompasses all things. We have to trust that His love goes to such great heights! As you read the last chapter, may you have strength to truly comprehend the height of God's love through Jesus Christ His Son.

Father, we pray that according to the riches of Your glory, that we would have the strength to comprehend that the height of Your love is beyond all measure (Ephesians 3:14-19).

Response:

"When peace, like a river, attendeth my way,
When sorrows like sea billows roll;
Whatever my lot, thou hast taught me to say,
It is well; it is well with my soul.

It is well with my soul,
It is well; it is well with my soul.

Though Satan should buffet, though trials should come,
Let this blest assurance control,
That Christ has regarded my helpless estate,
And hath shed his own blood for my soul.

My sin, oh, the bliss of this glorious thought!
My sin, not in part but the whole,
Is nailed to the cross, and I bear it no more,
Praise the Lord, praise the Lord, O my soul!

And, Lord, haste the day when my faith shall be sight,
The clouds be rolled back as a scroll;
The trump shall resound, and the Lord shall descend,
Even so, it is well with my soul."[11]

9

He Turned Me Into
Somebody Loved

"This is how God showed His love among us: He sent His one and only Son into the world that we might live through Him. This is love: not that we loved God, but that He loved us and sent His Son as an atoning sacrifice for our sins." -1 John 4:9-10

There's a song called "Somebody Loved" by the group "The Weepies." In the song, Deb Talan sings:

Rain turns the sand into mud.
Wind turns the trees into bone.
Stars turning high up above,
You turn me into somebody loved.[1]

This song is referring to a romantic kind of love. It makes me think of my wife, Jennifer. It is because of the fact that Jennifer loves me, that I'm someone loved. If it weren't for her love, I wouldn't be loved. She has turned me into "somebody loved" like the song says.

If you think about it, the greatest moments in a marriage are not those times when you feel like your spouse is so lucky to have you. This kind of attitude looks at and promotes self, saying things like, "Look at all I do around this house, and in this marriage. I do everything!" This is a prideful attitude and true romance cannot blossom in this kind of environment. The other kind of attitude of the heart is, "Wow! This person loves me, made a covenant to spend the rest of her life with me through sickness and health, rich or poor, for better or worse. I am a sinner and I frequently mess up, yet this person loves me still. I am somebody loved in spite of myself." This is a picture of humility, and a humble heart is what Christ calls us to have.

For the Christian, the beauty of what we've studied, in the length, breadth, depth and height of God's love, is ultimately seen by this truth: that Jesus Christ has turned us into somebody loved.[2] We are the lepers. We are the prodigals. We are the ones in the pit. We are the ones that struggle with the heights of evil. As Romans 5 says, we are the "ungodly," the "sinners," and the "enemies" of God (5:6, 8, 10). The beauty of the immeasurable love of Christ is not seen by patting ourselves on the back, telling each other how good we are, as if Christ is compelled to love us because of how adorable we are. No, the beauty of the immeasurable love of Christ is seen in the truth that He takes us in our filth, loves us, pays the penalty for our sins, and transforms us into people who bring Him glory.

The way we become the beloved children of God is through personal faith in Jesus Christ. The Bible says, "All who believed in His name, He gave the right to become the children of God" (John 1:12). This believing is not a work that man does in order to earn salvation; rather it is a gift of God. Ephesians 2:8-9 says, "For by grace you have been saved through faith. And this is not your own doing; it is the gift of God, not a result of works, so that no one may boast." Faith itself is a gift from God, and those who are His children "were born not of blood nor of the will of the flesh nor of the will of man, but of God" (John 1:13).

My desire is to be as clear as possible on this point. What I have written concerning our condition applies to every person. All people enter into this world with the cancerous problem of sin. We "were by nature children of wrath, like the rest of mankind" (Ephesians 2:3). While all people enter into the world as children of wrath because of sin, not all people are the children of God. The way the unearned love of Christ is poured freely upon us is by grace through faith. Romans 10:9-10 says, "If you confess with your mouth that Jesus is Lord and believe in your heart that God raised Him from the dead, you will be saved. For with the heart one believes and is justified, and with the mouth one confesses and is saved." The other side of this beautiful coin is the hard reality that those who don't believe in Jesus and don't confess Him as Lord and Savior will not be saved.

For this reason, we must turn our eyes upon the cross of Christ. The central and most concentrated place we see the love of God is here. It is in the intense suffering of Jesus on the cross that we see both our filth and His great love. The brutality of it displays my condition apart from Him. It shows what I deserved and how ugly my sin is. We tend to view ourselves as though we're not that bad. We like to think of sin in calculable terms. We place sins into categories, thinking that the dirty are those who drink, cuss, commit adultery or murder, but what about the stealthy nature of pride masquerading itself in mock humility? Do we fail to consider the ugliness of greed or lust within our hearts? What about our impure, selfish motives? The cross forces us to unmask our pretentious 'goodness' by putting on full display what our sins look like. However, just as the cross reveals our sin, so too does it radiate the love of God.

Beyond All Measure

"This is how God showed His love among us..." (1 John 4:9):

The cross displays the breadth of His love. "For God so loved the world that He gave His only Son, that whoever believes in Him should not perish but have eternal life" (John 3:16). There are no types of people that are out of bounds when it comes to His love. When Jesus was delivered over to the Roman soldiers to be crucified, there was another man who was set free. His name was Barabbas. He wasn't a good man. His crimes were insurrection and murder. The choice was given to the people as to who they wanted to be crucified, and they chose Jesus. This is what I refer to as the Gospel according to Barabbas. He should have been the one on the middle cross, yet Christ went in his place. He was set free and the One whom Pilate found no guilt deserving of death was brutally killed. We don't know the end of the story for Barabbas. Scripture doesn't tell us whether he believed in and received Jesus as the Christ, or if he rejected Him. The image of Jesus taking his place is still a beautiful reminder that Christ doesn't show love based on color, gender or age. Barabbas reminds us that at the cross there are no distinctions. "There is neither Jew nor Greek, there is neither slave nor free, there is neither male nor female, for you are all one in Christ Jesus" (Galatians 3:28). This is love beyond all measure.

"This is how God showed His love among us..." (1 John 4:9):

The cross reveals the length of His love. There is no sin that He can't forgive. Think about the thief on the cross. We don't know much about his crimes other than the fact that he was a thief and that he mocked Jesus (Matthew 27:44). Was he loved at all by any person? How did he end up such a criminal worthy of such a horrendous death? Yet Christ looks at him from His cross and says, "Today, you will be with Me in Paradise." The thief was turned into "somebody loved" because of Christ's love for him. "With You there is forgiveness!" (Psalm 130:4). At the cross we find that "as far as the east is from the west, so far does He remove our transgressions from us" (Psalm 103:12). You don't have to clean up first. This is love beyond all measure.

"This is how God showed His love among us..." (1 John 4:9):

The cross shows the depth of His love. "For we do not have a high priest who is unable to sympathize with our weaknesses, but one who in every respect has been tempted as we are, yet without sin" (Hebrews 4:15). The night before Jesus was crucified He prayed in the Garden of Gethsemane. He told His disciples to pray as well, but they fell asleep. He knew the intense suffering that awaited Him, and in His moment of greatest need, His disciples took a nap. He was alone. His anguish was so intense, His pit so deep, that His sweat became like great drops of blood. He knows what it is like to suffer. At the cross, we're reminded that there is no pain that we'll experience through which He hasn't already endured. This is love beyond all measure.

"This is how God showed His love among us..." (1 John 4:9):

The cross magnifies the height of His love. There has never been a greater evil than the crucifixion of God's Son. His veins were ruptured and His tendons were crushed. There were pangs of thirst. He breathed in, but with the inability to push Himself upward, exhaling became increasingly difficult. He endured mocking, spits to the face, cruelty and unbelief. "He was despised and rejected by men; a man of sorrows, and acquainted with grief" (Isaiah 53:3). Added to the physical pain was the spiritual pain of the sins of the world laid upon Him. He bore the wrath of God on our behalf, crying out, "My God, my God, why have You forsaken Me?" (Matthew 27:46). He took upon Himself the heights of evil so that we could be the sons of God. At the cross, "He disarmed the rulers and authorities and put them to open shame by triumphing over them in Him" (Colossians 2:15). There is no evil that goes unnoticed. The cross reminds us that He is the King, and He's won the victory. This is love beyond all measure.

The cross is the single most concentrated place we can see the love of God. It is there we're reminded that God's love is not measured in scoops of pleasant circumstances. His love is most clearly seen by His sacrificial death in our stead.

I Love You Too

"We love because He first loved us" (1 John 4:19).

When Jennifer journals her prayers to the Lord, she always writes at the closing, "I love You too." She does this as a reminder to her that she loves God because He first loved her. The love that God shows to us demands a response. There's no way we can just yawn it away as if it's no big deal. He laid down His life for us and now calls us the very children of God.

It reminds me of the story at the end of the Gospel of John where Jesus cooks breakfast for His disciples on the beach. This event takes place after He had been crucified, buried and raised from the dead. He had appeared to His disciples on a couple of occasions, but no longer walked with them daily. The setting of this story is that Peter and six other disciples go fishing, but come up empty-handed. Jesus shows up on the shore and calls out to them, "Do you have any fish?" (21:5). After they respond to the question with a disappointing "no," Jesus tells them to cast the net on the other side of the boat. They listen to Him and catch so many fish that they can't even drag them all aboard. They hadn't recognized Him up to this point, but they quickly realize this One on the shore is Jesus Himself. Peter in his excitement jumps over-board and swims to the shore to meet Him.

Upon reaching the shore, the disciples find that Jesus had already cooked fish for them. He invites them to have breakfast with Him, and what follows is a conversation with Peter focused on restoration. Days before, Peter had denied Jesus on three separate occasions. In love, Jesus goes to the cross to sacrifice Himself so that the Peters, lepers, prodigals, and people like you and I could have an eternal relationship with God. A love like this demands a response, and that's exactly what happens on the beach after finishing breakfast together.

> When they had finished breakfast, Jesus said to Simon Peter, "Simon, son of John, do you love Me more than these?" He said to him, "Yes, Lord; you know that I love you." He said to Him, "Feed my lambs" (21:15).

"Do you love Me more than these?" What does Jesus mean when He says, "more than these"? Is Jesus asking Peter if he loves Him more than the other disciples do? This would seem to be out of character for Jesus, since it would require Peter to answer the question in a way that compares his love for Christ with another's love for Christ. More likely, He's referring to the pile of fish that the disciples had just brought to shore. "Peter, do you love me more than these dead fish?" Catching fish was Peter's business. This was his vocation. Jesus reminds Peter of what he is to live for with this simple question, "Do you love me more than these?" In other words, are you willing to leave this behind and pursue the life to which I've called you? Do you treasure Me above all else?

Jesus asks the question to Peter three times, to which Peter responds with, "Lord, you know everything; you know that I love you" (John 21:17). This all happens after Peter has seen the lengths to which Jesus went to express His love, even enduring death on a cross. In response to the immeasurable love of Christ, Peter responds with, "I love you." Continuing on into the book of Acts, there is a visible difference between the Peter who denied Christ three times, and the one who boldly preaches Christ to thousands. Christ's love transformed him. He left dead fish to feed lambs.

Isn't this the response that our hearts should sing and shout? Doesn't His love for us demand a response? This is the purpose for which we have been created. In light of this, let us respond with love and praise to our God.

> For this reason, I bow my knees before the Father, from whom every family in heaven and on earth is named, that according to the riches of His glory He may grant you to be strengthened with power through His Spirit in your inner being, so that Christ may dwell in your hearts through faith-that you, being rooted and grounded in love, may have strength to comprehend with all the saints what is the breadth and length and height and depth, and to know the love of Christ that surpasses knowledge, that you may be filled with all the fullness of God.
>
> Now to Him who is able to do far more abundantly than all that we ask or think, according to the power at work within us, to Him be glory in the church and in Christ Jesus throughout all generations, forever and ever. Amen (Ephesians 3:14-21).

Oh the breadth and length and depth and height of Christ's love! Praying that together we'll have strength to comprehend a love that is beyond all measure to the praise of His glory!

Response:

"And can it be that I should gain
An interest in the Savior's blood?
Died He for me, who caused His pain—
For me, who Him to death pursued?
Amazing love! How can it be,
That Thou, my God, shouldst die for me?
Amazing love! How can it be,
That Thou, my God, shouldst die for me?

He left His Father's throne above
So free, so infinite His grace—
Emptied Himself of all but love,
And bled for Adam's helpless race:
'Tis mercy all, immense and free,
For O my God, it found out me!
'Tis mercy all, immense and free,
For O my God, it found out me!

Long my imprisoned spirit lay,
Fast bound in sin and nature's night;
Thine eye diffused a quickening ray—
I woke, the dungeon flamed with light;
My chains fell off, my heart was free,
I rose, went forth, and followed Thee.
My chains fell off, my heart was free,
I rose, went forth, and followed Thee.

No condemnation now I dread;
Jesus, and all in Him, is mine;
Alive in Him, my living Head,
And clothed in righteousness divine,
Bold I approach th'eternal throne,
And claim the crown, through Christ my own.
Bold I approach th'eternal throne,
And claim the crown, through Christ my own."[3]

Notes

Acknowledgments

[1] John Bunyan, *All Love's Excelling,* (Edinburgh: The Banner of Truth Trust, 1692).

Introduction

[1] John Owen, *A Puritan Golden Treasury*, compiled by I.D.E. Thomas, (Carlisle, PA: Banner of Truth, 2000) 175.

[2] Kathy Little, *How to Parent Your Adult Child* (Johnson City, TN: Kathy V. Little Publishing, 2001), 1.

[3] Kathy Little, *Loving Other People* (Johnson City, TN: Kathy V. Little Publishing, 2004), 1.

[4] Thomas Watson, *The Doctrine of Repentance* (Edinburgh: Banner of Truth Trust, repr. 1987), 63.

[5] Bunyan.

[6] D.A. Carson, *A Call to Spiritual Reformation,* (Grand Rapids, MI: Baker Books, 1992), 193-194.

[7] Steve Jeffery, Michael Ovey, Andrew Sach, *Pierced For Our Transgressions* (Wheaton, Illinois: Crossway Books, 2007), 151.

[8] D.A. Carson, *The Difficult Doctrine of the Love of God* (Leicester: IVP, 2000), 9-10.

[9] Henri Nouwen, *The Return of the Prodigal Son* (New York: Image Books, Doubleday, 1992), 42.

Part One: Think Long

[1] Mates of State, "Think Long," *Bring It Back*, 2006.

Chapter 1: How Far Away

[1] *Merriam-Webster Dictionary*.

[2] William Lane Craig, *Reasonable Faith* (Wheaton, Illinois: Crossway Books, 1984), xiv.

[3] See John Piper, *Desiring God* (Sisters, Oregon: Multnomah Publishers, 1986).

[4] Clara T. Williams, "Satisfied," 1875.

[5] Timothy Keller, *The Reason for God* (New York: Dutton, 2008), 46.

[6] Thomas Watson, *Doctrine of Repentance* (Edinburgh: Banner of Truth, 1988), 110.

Chapter 2: How Far His Reach

[1] Nouwen, 106-107.

[2] John Piper, *The Pleasures of God* (Sisters, Oregon: Multnomah Publishers, 2000), 189.

[3] Nouwen, 35.

[4] Edward Mote, "The Solid Rock," circa 1834.

[5] John Chapman, "Jesus, What A Friend For Sinners," 1910.

Part Two: Widespread

Chapter 3: How Widespread the Condition

[1] Ralph Venning, *The Sinfulness of Sin* (Edinburgh, Scotland, and Carlisle, PA: The Banner of Truth Trust, 1965, first published 1669), 31.
[2] E.W.G. Masterson, *Dictionary of Christ in the Gospels,* ed. James Hastings (Edinburgh: T & T Clark, 1908).
[3] J.C. Ryle, *Expository Thoughts on Mark* (Edinburgh: Banner of Truth Trust, repr. 1994), 21.
[4] Jerry Bridges, *Respectable Sins* (Colorado Springs: NavPress, 2007), 23.
[5] J.I. Packer, *Concise Theology* (Wheaton: Tyndale House Publishers, Inc., 1993), 82.
[6] *Westminster Confession IX.3.*
[7] Ray Comfort, "Hell's Best Kept Secret", 1982.

Chapter 4: How Widespread the Cure

[1] Daniel Fuller, *Gospel and Law: Contrast or Continuum?* (Grand Rapids: Eerdmans, 1980), 117-119.
[2] Ken Gire, *Moments With The Savior* (Grand Rapids: Zondervan Publishing House, 1998), 115.
[3] Brian H. Edwards, *Through Many Dangers: The Story of John Newton* (Welwyn, England: Eurobooks, 1980), 191.

[4] John Piper, *The Pleasures of God* (Sisters, Oregon: Multnomah Publishers, 2000), 214-215.

[5] Louie Giglio, *I Am Not But I Know I Am* (Colorado Springs: Multnomah Books, 2005), 13.

[6] This phrase is from the song "Remedy" from the album *Remedy* by The David Crowder Band, 2007.

[7] Crowder.

Part Three: How Deep

Chapter 5: How Deep the Pit

[1] C.S. Lewis, *A Grief Observed* (New York: HarperCollins Publishers, 1961), 6.

[2] F.W. Faber, quoted in Ralph G. Turnbull, *A Minister's Obstacles* (1946; repr. Grand Rapids: Baker, 1972), 97.

[3] Coty Pinckney, "When God Doesn't Answer," a sermon on Psalm 77. Community Bible Church, Williamstown, MA. 1996.

[4] William Cowper, "God Moves In A Mysterious Way," 1774.

Chapter 6: "How Firm the Foundation"

[1] Helmut Thielicke, "The Theater of Incarnation," *The Book of Jesus,* ed. Calvin Miller (Nashville, Tennessee: Broadman & Holman Publishers, 1996), 222-223.

[2] C.S. Lewis, *Mere Christianity* (New York: Macmillan, 1960), 119.

[3] Andrew Murray, quoted in Amy Carmichael, *Though the Mountains Shake* (New York: Loizeaux Bros., 1946), 12.

[4] C.J. Mahaney, *Living the Cross Centered Life* (Sisters, Oregon: Multnomah Publishers, 2006), 98.

[5] Bernhard Schumacher, "How Firm A Foundation," 1931.

Part Four: Such Great Heights

[1] From a title of a song by The Postal Service, "Such Great Heights," *Give Up*, 2003.

Chapter 7: "How Long O Lord?"

[1] David Wells, *The Courage to Be Protestant,* (Grand Rapids: William B. Eerdmans Publishing Company, 2008), 101.

[2] David Hume, *Dialogues Concerning Natural Religion,* part X in *Writings on Religion,* ed. Antony Flew (Chicago: Open Court, 1996), 261.

[3] Keller, 22.

[4] Michael Peterson, *God and Evil,* (Boulder Colorado: Westview Press, 1998), 1.

[5] Millard Erickson, *Christian Theology,* 2nd ed. (Grand Rapids: Baker, 1998), 437.

[6] Allan Laing, "Wave that beggared my belief," (Glasgow: *The Herald,* January 4, 2005), 14.

[7] Statistics as reported on www.globalissues.org.

[8] Fyodor Dostoevsky, *The Brothers Karamazov,* quoted in *The Problem of Evil,* ed. Michael L.

Peterson (Notre Dame, Indiana: University of Notre Dame Press, 1992), 64.

[9] Paul Williams and Barry Cooper, *If You Could Ask God One Question,* (New Malden, Surrey, UK: The Good Book Company Ltd., 2007), 91-92.

[10] Gregory Boyd, *Is God To Blame?* (Downers Grove, IL: InterVarsity, 2003), 125.

Chapter 8: How High His Love

[1] http://www.thefreedictionary.com/overtop

[2] Harold Kushner, *When Bad Things Happen to Good People* (New York: Avon Books, 1981), 43.

[3] John Flavel, *The Mystery of Providence,* (Edinburgh: The Banner of Truth Trust, 1678), 27.

[4] Ibid, 22.

[5] Dorothy L. Sayers, "The Triumph of Easter", *Creed or Chaos* (Methuen 1954).

[6] Stephen John Wykstra, "Rowe's Noseeum Arguments From Evil in The Evidential Argument From Evil, (Bloomington and Indianapolis: Indiana University Press, 1996), 126-128.

[7] Jerry Bridges, *Is God Really In Control?* (Colorado Springs: Navpress, 2006), 26.

[8] Charles Spurgeon, "God's Providence", a sermon preached at New Park Street Chapel, Southwark. Published in 1908.

[9] Wykstra, 129.

[10] David Wilcox, "Hold It Up To The Light," *Big Horizon*, 1994.

[11] Horatio G. Spafford, "It Is Well With My Soul", 1873.

Conclusion: He Turned Me Into Somebody Loved

[1] The Weepies, "Somebody Loved," *Happiness*, 2003.

[2] This is not a theological following of N.T. Wright's view of justification. We are justified not because He transforms us through sanctification, but rather because of the imputation of our sin to Christ and the imputation of Christ's righteousness to us.

[3] Charles Wesley, "And Can It Be?," 1738.

Printed in the United States
140956LV00001B/2/P

9 781607 913498